The Rockwell Heist

The extraordinary
theft of seven Norman
Rockwell paintings

and a phony
Renoir—and the
20-year chase
for their recovery,

BOREALIS
BOOKS

The
Rockwell Heist

from the Midwest
through Europe
and South America

Bruce Rubenstein

The publication of this book was supported by the Ken and Nina Rothchild Endowed Fund for Business History.

Borealis Books is an imprint of the Minnesota Historical Society Press.

www.mhspress.org

The Minnesota Historical Society Press is a member of the Association of American University Presses.

Manufactured in the United States of America

10 9 8 7 6 5 4 3 2 1

♾ The paper used in this publication meets the minimum requirements of the American National Standard for Information Sciences—Permanence for Printed Library Materials, ANSI Z39.48-1984.

International Standard Book Number

ISBN: 978-0-87351-890-1 (cloth)
ISBN: 978-0-87351-896-3 (e-book)

Library of Congress Cataloging-in-Publication Data

Rubenstein, Bruce, 1938–
    The Rockwell heist / Bruce Rubenstein.
        pages cm
    Summary: "In 1979 seven Norman Rockwell paintings and a supposed Renoir, later discovered to be a forgery, were stolen from Elayne's Gallery in St. Louis Park. It is still the biggest theft in Minnesota history, and no one was ever convicted for the crime. This is the story of the theft, the investigation, and the twenty-year quest to return the art to its rightful owners."—Provided by publisher.
    Includes bibliographical references.
    ISBN 978-0-87351-890-1 (hardback) — ISBN 978-0-87351-896-3 (e-book)
    1. Art thefts—Minnesota—Edina. 2. Rockwell, Norman, 1894–1978. I. Title.
    N8795.3.U6R83 2013
    364.16'2875913—dc23
                                                                2012044691

The Rockwell Heist

1

ON THE EVENING OF FEBRUARY 16, 1978, MORE THAN
five hundred people gathered at Elayne Galleries in St.
Louis Park, Minnesota, to drink champagne, celebrate
Norman Rockwell's eighty-fourth birthday, and maybe
purchase some art.

It was the largest show of Rockwell's paintings ever
held in a private gallery. The plans originally included
an appearance by Rockwell, but the artist couldn't attend. He was bedridden, and would die nine months
later. Nevertheless, he was a major presence at the show.
Eight of his original paintings were on display, as were
many of his signed, limited-edition lithographs.

A dock scene attributed to the French Impressionist
Pierre-Auguste Renoir was the co-feature. It had a crack
extending from the edge into the artist's signature that
diminished its value somewhat, but it was still worth
plenty. Altogether the exhibition was an impressive ar-
ray of valuable art, well publicized and well attended.

NORMAN ROCKWELL
RETROSPECTIVE

FEBRUARY 18-MARCH 5

Unlike many gallery owners, Elayne and Russ Lindberg had taken steps to prevent a robbery. They had hired a contractor to make the premises secure. He installed an audio-sonic alarm and a "theft proof" lock. They hired the Pinkerton Agency to guard the premises for the duration of the show.

The Lindbergs had gained a nationwide reputation for handling Rockwell's work. Six of his paintings were on loan for the show, but two others belonged to the

SPECIAL PRIVATE OPENING
FEBRUARY 16, 5-9 pm

"Because Rockwell breathed affection into his paintings, they aroused affection in the heart of the beholder, and one was dull indeed who did not comprehend that the Common Man was a quite uncommon fellow."

February marks the 84th birthday of America's most loved living artist, Norman Rockwell. In order to celebrate the occasion, we have assembled the nation's largest display of Norman Rockwell, in a private gallery. The show includes eight original paintings, a complete collection of his magazine covers, and a film.

You are specially invited to attend the private opening of the show Thursday, February 16, 5-9 p.m. Join us for some champagne and birthday cake, expertly designed by Byerly Foods.

Enjoy a walk through 50 years of America's history, so lovingly recorded by Norman Rockwell.

The show will be on display through March 5th.

elayne

The invitation to the show at Elayne Galleries at which the paintings were stolen. This special invitation went out to a list of more than five hundred gallery clients.

gallery, and the opening attracted the kind of collectors who might be interested in buying them.

"It was a good time to be in the business. Art as an investment was becoming very popular in the 1970s," says the gallery owners' daughter, Bonnie Lindberg, now an estate appraiser in St. Louis Park.

Bonnie was twenty-two when the Rockwell party took place, blond and pretty, with a dazzling smile. Her mother, a publicity hound who knew how to stage an event, made sure her daughter was around at openings. Her presence was one small detail of a marketing plan that was part buzz and part blitzkrieg. Mailings had gone to clients and potential clients, and circulars had been handed to people on the street and tucked under the windshields of parked cars. There were blurbs in newspapers, and word of mouth had spread via a network that reached art collectors and artists, of course, but also Elayne Lindberg's former colleagues from law enforcement and probably a few shoplifters she had collared during her days as a store detective. Elayne's knack for turning an opening into a well-orchestrated extravaganza had boosted her gallery into the top echelon of the local art scene by 1978. Later that year, a show at Elayne Galleries would be billed as "the largest one-time exhibit ever" of the Minnesota-born artist LeRoy Neiman's work. It featured more than seventy

Elayne Lindberg, her daughter Bonnie, and the sheet cake baked for the opening of the Rockwell show

original paintings, prints and posters, plus the artist himself, sporting his trademark moustache. A delegation of boosters from the town of Leroy, Minnesota, arrived about the time the crowd peaked and presented Neiman with the keys to their city.

The Rockwell bash was a gala evening by all accounts, despite an unnerving incident the day before. Three men who didn't look like art lovers had strolled into the gallery. Extra help had been hired for the show, and the place was bustling with preparations, but the general demeanor of the three, and the fact that one of them didn't bother taking off his sunglasses as he viewed paintings, got everybody's attention.

"Things more or less came to a halt," Elayne Lindberg later told investigators.

The men had some pointed questions to ask about the value of various works of art. Russ Lindberg, normally affable and outgoing, was short with them. He took note of their "bold" attitude and their physical appearance.

After splitting up and browsing awhile, the men gathered near the Renoir, where they were overheard discussing what measures might be in place to protect it. Russ thought they were paying particular attention to the windows and doors. They stayed about twenty-five minutes. When they left, Russ followed them outside and wrote down the license number of their car, a white 1976 Chevy Impala.

"I think he wanted them to know he'd spotted them," says his son, Gary, thirty-five at the time, now an author living in Chanhassen, Minnesota.

The impression the incident left was of three workmanlike robbers who knew exactly what they wanted and were casing the gallery for entrance and exit routes. Elayne Lindberg called them "cocky."

After the party ended and the gallery closed for the night, seven of the Rockwell paintings and the Renoir were stolen. The thieves punched the "theft proof" lock and cut the electrical cord that powered the alarm. The ease with which they foiled the security system indicated that they were either very skilled or had some familiarity with its components. The art was estimated to be worth $500,000 when it was stolen, and even though one of the paintings has since proven to be a fake, their net value has mushroomed to more than $1 million now, making it the biggest robbery in the state's history. The crime was never solved, but the Rockwell paintings were recovered twenty-two years later, after they had been bought and sold on three continents.

The FBI files and interviews with attorneys and others indicate that the theft was planned at the last moment. The perpetrators evidently either checked out an opportunity spotted by someone they were inclined to blow off and discovered it was real or they got a contract for a rush job from organized crime figures on the East Coast.

A last-minute hitch prevented them from taking one of the paintings they had targeted, but they got away cleanly with the others. It looked like they had hit the jackpot. The problem was monetization, but there is a lively market for stolen art and in 1978 it was evolving fast.

Today, according to Interpol, the global traffic in stolen art is an illicit commerce exceeded only by drugs and black market arms sales.

2

IN FICTION AND FILM, ART THEFT IS DEPICTED AS A TRADE plied by master criminals who plan their robberies meticulously in order to foil elaborate security measures. In reality, most art is pilfered opportunistically by thieves who know an easy score when they spot one. Works that are marketable but not well known make up the bulk of stolen art, but more than $5 billion changes hands annually in the trade, an average fattened periodically by the theft of a masterpiece or, more often, several masterpieces. The lack of security at places where great art is displayed—museums, public buildings, galleries, and collectors' homes—continually amazes investigators who specialize in such cases, all the more so because the cost of insuring masterpieces is astronomical and most owners pass entirely or insure for a fraction of value.

The twelve paintings by Rembrandt, Degas, Manet, and Vermeer, plus a Shang Dynasty vase, that were stolen in 1990 from the Isabella Stewart Gardner Museum in Boston—worth an estimated $200 million—were not insured against theft at all. It couldn't have been because the curators never considered the possibility. Art journals and museum newsletters routinely take note of art thefts, and they've always had plenty to discuss.

The Mona Lisa was stolen in 1911. Like many art thefts, it was an inside job, and the painting was recovered from a museum guard's home in 1913. In 1961, Goya's "Portrait of the Duke of Wellington" was stolen from England's National Gallery. Two paintings by Piero della Francesca and a Raphael were stolen from the Ducal Palace in Urbino, Italy, in 1975. In 2002, two Van Goghs were stolen from the Van Gogh Museum in Amsterdam. In 2006, paintings by Dali, Picasso, Matisse, and Monet were taken from the Chácara do Céu Museum in Rio de Janeiro.

A 1988 theft in New York netted eighteen paintings, including two by the early Renaissance Florentine, Fra Angelico. It took place at the Manhattan branch of the London dealer Colnaghi's and illustrated something art thieves had figured out a decade or so earlier: the value of works on display in private homes and galleries often rivals those at museums, and the security is even worse.

In 2012, works by Vermeer, Cezanne, Picasso, Matisse, and Van Gogh were all listed on the Art Loss Register (an authoritative database of missing art used by museums, art dealers, and law enforcement), among them the loot from a theft at the Musée d'Art Moderne de la Ville de Paris, in which five paintings worth $123 million were stolen. At the time of the theft at the Musée, an alarm system had been broken for three months. External cameras meant to catch would-be robbers in the act were focused on the roof, but the thief or thieves broke a window and entered unnoticed. Guards were said to be napping. Musée officials refused to discuss how much insurance they had on the paintings, leading most observers to conclude they had none.

3

THE BUILDING AT 6111 EXCELSIOR BOULEVARD WAS ELAYNE
Galleries' second location. Six years before the robbery,
it had opened in a St. Louis Park storefront, with an
inventory of European oil paintings that Russ Lindberg
had acquired in connection with his interior decorating business. Sales were brisk, and the Lindbergs soon
decided they needed more space. The mall where they
moved wasn't exactly where one would expect to find
an art gallery, but it fit Elayne Lindberg's unconven-
tional approach to the business.

"Mom was all about sales," says Bonnie Lindberg,
"and she wasn't shy when it came to publicity. She'd
mail out circulars to everyone she could think of. She
even put them under the windshield wipers of cars
when we were having a show."

The robbery was carefully planned and methodically executed. Only the most valuable pieces were taken.
Investigators assumed that the three men who came to

the gallery the day before were the thieves, but the possibility that they were just three guys who wandered in because somebody put a leaflet on their windshield could never be totally discounted. That was one of the frustrating things about the case.

The Pinkerton guard was missing when the theft took place. "No one has ever figured out where he was, or why he wasn't at the gallery," says Bonnie. According to FBI records, there was some dispute about whether he had been instructed to stay on the premises or to patrol every half hour for the duration of the show.

It was the guard who discovered the theft at 12:30 AM and phoned 911. Investigators surmised that the thieves made a hurried exit when a lookout signaled the guard's return.

The St. Louis Park police initially pieced together a burglary that took about fifteen minutes. Evidence at the scene indicated that one more painting, another Rockwell, was ticketed for theft, but the thieves fled without it. A black garbage bag was left on the gallery floor. The investigators theorized that the missing paintings were taken out in the same type of bag, and the bag left behind would have been used when the thieves grabbed the last Rockwell.

The plate number of the white Chevy was checked.

It had been bought and sold three times the previous month. The only owner of record who could be traced was quickly cleared of any involvement.

Eight paintings were stolen. They were:

- "Date/Cowgirl" and "Date/Cowboy," an oil study by Rockwell for a 1949 *Saturday Evening Post* cover executed as a diptych, owned by the gallery (collectively called "the date paintings" and treated as one work, which explains why news reports and investigators' files sometimes say seven Rockwell paintings were stolen);
- four Rockwell paintings owned by the Brown & Bigelow Company of St. Paul: "The Spirit of 1976," "No Swimming," "Summer," and "Winter";
- a Rockwell titled "She's My Baby," owned by Robert Horvath of Minneapolis;
- the untitled Renoir, owned by Robert "Buddy" Verson of St. Paul.

(All the Rockwells were executed as studies for reproduction, either as a magazine cover or a calendar illustration, and were untitled by the artist. They sometimes came to be known by more than one title later.)

Horvath and Verson had been gallery clients for a while. Horvath bought "She's My Baby" from Elayne

"Date/Cowgirl"

"Date/Cowboy"

"The Spirit of 1976"

"No Swimming"

"Summer"

Galleries, and they had both purchased signed Rockwell lithographs.

The gallery's diptych was insured for $35,000. A rider was written on the gallery's policy insuring Brown & Bigelow's four paintings for $90,000. Horvath's Rockwell and Verson's Renoir were not covered by the rider. Both men had been cautioned to insure their paintings but hadn't done so.

By 3:30 AM on February 17, three hours after the theft

"Winter"

"She's My Baby"

Untitled "Renoir"

was discovered, police had issued a report of a "half-million-dollar robbery." It mentioned the Rockwells but said the Renoir was the most valuable painting stolen. It noted that the perpetrators confined their activities to the north end of the gallery where the Renoir and the Rockwells were hanging and apparently knew exactly what they were after. It included Russ Lindberg's description of the three suspicious men, all white males, who are referred to as suspects in the FBI files.

Suspect one was five feet eleven inches, approximately 170 pounds, well dressed, about forty years old, with a hook nose, a dark complexion, and dark hair. He "looked Italian" and "gave the impression that he was the leader."

Suspect two was in his late thirties, about six feet, with sandy-colored collar-length hair, knit slacks, and sharply pointed, alligator-skin cowboy boots. He had wires on his teeth and scars on his upper and lower lips "as if he had recently been in an accident." He wore a black trench coat. He wandered all over the gallery and kept popping back and forth, seemingly to report on something to suspect one.

Suspect three was over six feet as well, a little older than the other two, with graying brown hair and wearing a three-quarter-length "pieced" leather coat. He stood off by himself most of the time and said little.

The robbery was big news in the Twin Cities. "I remember there was a lot of talk that it was an inside job," says Minneapolis attorney Thomas E. Bauer, who was a Hennepin County prosecutor at the time.

The FBI took a keen interest in the case. They pursued it vigorously for a while and developed the only real theory that ever emerged. According to their analysis, someone with an insider's knowledge of the gallery, and the Rockwell show, conspired with professional burglars to commit the crime. They also related it to the activities of an organized crime ring operating out of Miami that was under investigation for selling fake art.

There was a sound basis for their theory. It fit with evidence they already had and more evidence they would soon discover. Furthermore, just about all art thefts are related to organized crime in some way, even if the involvement begins after the theft.

An hour after the initial report was released, a St. Louis Park detective on the overnight shift received a phone call from "a gentleman who identified himself as a full-time art dealer who did not want at this time to give his name or get involved."

The FBI files refer to him as Terrance W. Huberg, owner of Antiques Americana in Bethel, Minnesota. Huberg had been in his car when he heard about the crime on the radio. He told the detective that if the Renoir was the one he thought it was, it depicted a dock scene and had a five-inch crack running diagonally from the border through Renoir's signature. He had heard that it had recently been sold.

Several months before, sellers from Miami had made a concerted effort to persuade Huberg to buy the painting, which included an appraisal from Rikki's Art Studios in Miami claiming it was worth $125,000. The initial price was $50,000; the owner of record was a Miami resident of Cuban extraction. Huberg had a buyer promising to pay him $140,000 if he could prove the painting was genuine, and he sent photos along with a written description to an expert on French Impressionism at the Hammer Galleries in New York. He was told it was a fake. Not only did it lack Renoir's distinctive, streaky style of brushwork, but Renoir was known to be living inland at the time it was allegedly painted and concentrating solely on landscapes. Huberg declined to buy the painting. A few weeks later, he was told he could buy it for $15,000. He assumed this meant that word had gotten out that the painting was a fake, and a "fire sale" was on.

The FBI was already investigating the Cuban. His name is blacked out of the files, but a document written by a confederate of his dated February 8, 1978, refers to him as Rolando—last name unintelligible, but possibly Aherene.

Huberg gave the FBI a translation of a notarized document, originally in Spanish, purporting to detail the painting's provenance. In it, someone whose name is redacted in the FBI file claims to be the sole owner of the painting, which to his knowledge was painted by Renoir.

"This painting was bought by me approximately in the year 1958 from [redacted] who bought it from [redacted] who reported to him that it has been in her possession since the beginning of 1946. That same year it was brought into Cuba from Spain. This painting has been mine since approximately the year 1958 and has been kept and stored in Cuba since those years."

4

THE ROBBERY AT ELAYNE GALLERIES WAS WELL PUBLI-
cized. Several news stories described the three men
who visited the gallery the day before. Investigators
braced themselves for a deluge of tips and told the
Lindbergs to do the same. They weren't disappointed.

Phone calls offering information and theories came
from Lodi, California; Denver, Colorado; and Golden,
Colorado. An anonymous tip was traced to the phone
inmates used to make long-distance calls at Folsom
Prison, in California. A copy of the sign-up sheet on
the day the tip was received was provided to investigators. The prisoners were questioned, but none admitted making the call.

A woman from the Minneapolis neighborhood of
Camden said that a man had stayed at her boyfriend's
apartment for a while—"kind of a crazy guy with a
scarred face, who scared the hell out of the other resi-
dents"—and she was pretty sure he was one of the

thieves. He had moved to Colorado shortly after the gallery was robbed.

An anonymous caller said his father was the thief. The call was traced to a man who admitted making it to embarrass his father. The caller passed a polygraph test regarding the theft.

A man who had been to the gallery the day before the theft called to say that he was not involved in the crime. He'd just dropped by to see a LeRoy Neiman painting that was on display there. He said he liked Neiman's work, especially "those golf paintings."

A phone tip came in concerning a Norman Rockwell enthusiast in Michigan, who allegedly commissioned forged Rockwell posters. The tipster said the Rockwell enthusiast had mentioned the show at Elayne's.

A man who had recently been released from the St. Cloud prison fingered two former inmates for the robbery. One of them was residing at a halfway house in the Twin Cities. The informant offered to get in touch with his old prison mates and elicit some further information. He was homeless but told investigators that if they wanted to chat with him he could often be found at the Lyndale Diner.

A tipster said that one of the perpetrators hung out at the Barracks Bar on North Clark Street in Chicago.

A minor figure in the Minneapolis underworld contacted the FBI. He claimed that a thief from Chicago had approached him about participating in the Elayne Galleries heist about a month before it occurred. Agents met with him at a downtown coffee shop. He opened the conversation by saying that he wanted the "bugs" the FBI had placed on his vehicle removed. He explained that he was living in the vehicle, a 1971 Dodge Dart, and the bugs disturbed his sleep in some unspecified way. When the agents reminded him why the meeting had been set up, he said that he told the thief that he could not possibly entertain an offer to participate in the Elayne Galleries robbery because he

Elayne Galleries, the scene of the crime

had recently had a religious experience and considered himself "born again." The FBI later concluded that the thief he named actually participated in the robbery, but the informant had been lying about being contacted by him.

Psychics stopped by the gallery regularly, either offering their services for a fee or providing gratis information about the paintings' whereabouts. The first anniversary of the theft prompted a newspaper article and some television reports. The next day, a tip was received from someone who had recently been released from a mental institution. The paintings never left the building, she told investigators. They were hidden between the ceiling and the roof beams.

"A couple of agents came and tore into our ceiling because of that one," says Bonnie. "They were pretty apologetic when they didn't find anything."

Not all of the tips came from crackpots. Less than three weeks after the robbery, the Minneapolis police received what they called "credible information" that a well-known underworld figure was in on the job. He supposedly brought an accomplice from out of town with him.

A few days later, the FBI was contacted by the same man. He told them two well-known thieves whose names are redacted, one from Chicago and one from the Twin Cities, were "good for the job." This tipster would keep in touch with investigators for years.

It was reasonable to assume that organized crime was involved. It is extremely difficult to monetize stolen art that is well known, but mobsters have a standard method: they sit on it for a long time, then contact the owner or the insurer and threaten to destroy it if an exorbitant demand for cash is not met quickly. Apparently it works often enough to make it worth a try. If that fails, the piece often disappears into a stolen-art network in Europe that has been around in one form or another since the Renaissance.

5

IMMEDIATELY AFTER THE THEFT, THE FBI IDENTIFIED three gallery insiders who might have contacts with professional burglars, and—either through them or independently—with organized crime.

Suspect one was Bob Horvath, the owner of one of the stolen Rockwells, who had done extensive business with Elayne Galleries. There was a federal investigation into his affairs in progress at the time of the theft, and it involved money laundering, the kind of activity that might connect him to the crime. Evidence presented in the court case alleged the following chain of events:

In October 1975, a colleague of the Horvath brothers, Thomas O'Shaughnessy, drove a truck onto the beach at Folly Cove, on the Massachusetts coast. A few minutes later, a boat nosed ashore. O'Shaughnessy and a man named Dawson unloaded the cargo, a holdful of marijuana. The Horvaths had previously paid Dawson $40,000 for the weed.

O'Shaughnessy drove the truck to Minneapolis. It was one of several loads belonging to the Horvaths that were brought to the Twin Cities over a five-year period. Court records refer to one of those deals as "a million-dollar transaction."

About a year after the Folly Cove caper, O'Shaughnessy took up residence for a while in a motel in Ardmore, Oklahoma. By then he was under surveillance. His activities led the feds to believe that something illegal was in the works, and it might occur at a nearby airport. On December 30, 1976, police seized two aircraft and four trucks containing 17,000 pounds of marijuana at an airport near Ardmore. The occupants of the trucks were arrested.

Neither the Horvaths nor O'Shaughnessy were in Ardmore when the bust took place, and they did not stand trial in connection with the seizure, but it was cited as "a likely source of income" when the Horvath brothers, O'Shaughnessy, and a lawyer named Robert Malone stood trial for tax evasion in 1982. According to a summary of the case, "The Horvaths were in the business of distributing marijuana from 1975 through 1979. In addition to failing to report income from this illegal venture, the Horvaths allegedly made various purchases with cash through other parties under fictitious names, or through corporations, to conceal both their income and its sources." Essentially, they were caught for money laundering.

O'Shaughnessy, a jack of all trades, was implicated in several of those transactions. One involved a $25,000 investment in a phantom oil company, with O'Shaughnessy serving as middleman. Another was the purchase of a home by Bob Horvath, with O'Shaughnessy acting as a real estate agent. Cashier's checks from fictitious remitters were used in both deals.

Starting in 1976, the Horvaths' money-laundering activities allegedly involved their high school buddy Robert Malone, who was practicing law in Minneapolis. Malone's first task was collecting payments against an undocumented loan Bob Horvath claimed he had made to the owner of Spanky's Saloon, in downtown Minneapolis. Malone deposited the payments in a bank account, which was characterized in court records by what it was not—neither a trust account nor a savings account with a beneficiary.

On two occasions, Paul Horvath brought Malone checks that he said were the proceeds of gold transactions. Malone deposited them in trust accounts, the ownership records of which "made no reference to the Horvaths." Malone later made withdrawals from those accounts and delivered the money to the Horvaths.

Malone testified against the Horvaths at their tax evasion trial. After his testimony, he was acquitted of all charges. The Horvaths and O'Shaughnessy were convicted.

Much of the evidence used at trial against Bob Horvath was collected while the investigation of the art theft at Elayne Galleries was active and shared with agents pursuing that case. The art theft investigators considered the possibility that Horvath bought and sold art to launder money—and may have set up the theft of his own Rockwell.

Within days, they decided that he had nothing to do with the theft. The record is mum on how that conclusion was reached, but the fact that the painting he lost was not insured must have been a factor.

Horvath threatened to sue the gallery for the loss of his painting, but never did. "If I remember correctly, the statute of limitations passed while he was in prison," says Minneapolis defense attorney Joe Friedberg.

6

SUSPECT TWO WAS THE ULTIMATE INSIDER AT ELAYNE Galleries, Elayne Lindberg, a self-invented dynamo of a woman whose occupation before she went into the art business put her in contact with thieves and familiarized her with the flow of stolen goods in the Twin Cities.

Elayne was born in Browerville, Minnesota, moved to Minneapolis with her parents during the Depression, and met Russ Lindberg when he stopped by a grocery store in their neighborhood. They married in 1942 and started a family four years later, after Russ was discharged from the navy. She owed her vocation to an epiphany she experienced at a difficult point in her life.

Russ was an outgoing guy who loved the spotlight and tended to overshadow his wife. He was a musician, a songwriter, and a magician. He even preached at an Evangelical church for a while.

"My mother was a stay-at-home mom until I was in

junior high school," says her daughter, Bonnie, "but she was always involved with whatever Dad was doing on one level or another. Dad had an interior decorating business and many other interests and side careers. He played in a Dixieland band, he was a film writer and director, a songwriter—he even became a performing magician for a time. He'd do magic shows, and Mom would go with him as his assistant. He'd make her disappear. He'd saw her in half."

Elayne was small—five feet one inch—and pretty, ideal as a magician's assistant, except for one thing. While she loved her husband dearly, she hated being anyone's assistant. She was determined to find her own niche, and as soon as her daughter was old enough to take care of herself, she set out to do so.

It was a sobering experience. As she put it in the introduction to a book she wrote, *The Power of Positive Handwriting,* "I had a long list of 'if only's' in my life, and it grew longer with each unsuccessful interview."

She finally found a job, but a menial one. "So there I was," she wrote, "working as a bus girl in a cafeteria. Was this the lowest I could sink? No. Two months later I was fired for not cleaning the salt and pepper shakers properly. . . . I wallowed in self pity and mused about my many inadequacies."

A friend who wanted to pry her out of the doldrums

took her to a lecture by Josephine Nash, a self-styled "graphotherapist" who claimed she could solve people's problems through handwriting analysis. Each member of the audience was asked to write a note on a pre-numbered card. Nash promised that after the lecture she would give a short, personal (but public) analysis of each person based on those notes. Elayne drew number twelve.

"The prospect of this roomful of strangers being told the murky secrets of my personality made me want to disappear into my chair," wrote Elayne. Nevertheless, she composed a note and handed it in.

To Elayne's surprise, Nash had an uplifting message. Number twelve had all the qualities necessary to succeed and only one trait, hypersensitivity, that was holding her back. Nash demonstrated the handwriting stroke that revealed this trait on a blackboard and then offered some free graphotherapy. By changing that stroke, the undesirable trait itself could be altered. It was Nash's contention that people could remake their personality by methodically changing their handwriting.

Elayne took that advice to heart. "I'd found another direction for my life," she wrote. "I became a certified grapho-analyst and a pioneer in the field of questioned documents."

The documents in question were usually checks.

Elayne became a grapho-analytical consultant with metro-area police departments, county attorney's offices, and the Minnesota attorney general's office. Prosecutors had enough confidence in her forensic capabilities to use her as an expert witness on many occasions. She also identified forged checks and credit account forgeries at Dayton's department store, and she used her skills in graphology to analyze the characters of executive-level job applicants at Dayton's and other companies.

Eventually she landed a job in the Dayton Hudson Corporation's security department, and for a while she worked as a store detective. By then the failed bus girl who spent her days musing about her inadequacies had transformed herself into a can-do personality—someone who was confident in her abilities to spot a forgery, divine from a person's handwriting whether he was C-suite material, and interrupt a department store theft with a minimum of fuss.

Nevertheless, she was a tiny woman, and her ability to collar a thief rested on a social compact that was unraveling fast in downtown Minneapolis in the 1960s.

"I think the last straw was when a guy pulled a gun on her," says Bonnie. "She realized her life was on the line, and she began looking for a new career."

The Lindbergs had a knack for turning their passions into cash, and they had always been attracted to the arts. Russ had accumulated a large inventory of European oil paintings in connection with his decorating business. They decided to use them to open an art gallery.

"Dad had chosen those paintings, but it was really her project from the beginning," says Bonnie Lindberg. "She was the prime mover. That's why they called it Elayne Galleries."

Elayne brought the same entrepreneurial zeal and some of the same skills to the art business that she brought to the questioned-documents trade. She studied the methodology of art authentication, became a member of the American Art Association of Appraisers, and was certified by the Academy of Art Conservation. But it was her social gifts that made the business thrive. She enjoyed promoting shows and making sales— working with people generally—and she developed an easy rapport with many artists.

"She genuinely loved people," says Gary Lindberg, "particularly people who needed encouragement."

As a result, there was rarely if ever an artist who walked into Elayne Galleries and didn't come out feeling good about the experience, whether he or she ended up showing there or not.

"How would I describe Elayne? Warm, outgoing, supportive. She never let me down, that's for sure," says Kevin Daniel, an artist known for wildlife and western scenes. "She and Russ were heavy hitters in the art scene around here. I met her at a show in downtown Minneapolis, and pretty soon I was showing with them."

The Lindbergs and Kevin Daniel entered into a joint venture. A local publisher produced limited-edition, numbered prints of Daniel's work. He signed them and sold them exclusively through Elayne Galleries. The venture was a success, and it introduced the Lindbergs to the advantages of the limited-edition market.

"She was such a lively person, a real sweetheart," says Ron Ringling, who bought limited-edition Rockwells from the gallery. "She had charisma."

Elayne was quick to recognize commercial potential where other gallery owners missed it. For example, she leaped at the chance to show original drawings by Richard Guindon, a cartoonist who had developed a reputation based on his work in an influential counter-culture magazine, *The Realist*, before he was hired by the *Minneapolis Tribune* in 1968.

At the *Tribune*, Guindon developed a stock repertoire of quirky types from all walks of midwestern life—sheet-metal workers commiserating over three-two beers, ice fishermen wearing goofy caps with ear laps, rap-parlor hookers with skinny legs and platform shoes. His cartoons became a mainstay on the paper's editorial page.

In 1977, after the paper published a book of his gag panels that sold out in a matter of days (and balked at printing more copies even though it was back-ordered in quantity), Guindon realized that his original drawings were saleable, too. He had to fish many of them out of a wastebasket in the *Tribune's* graphics department, but over time he assembled a large collection and began looking for a venue to show them.

"I wanted to find the right gallery, and the name Elayne Galleries came up as soon as I started tossing the idea around," says Guindon. "But when I first walked in the place to size it up, I was a little taken back. What I saw on the walls was an odd combination of motel art, along with some more serious stuff."

Whatever misgivings he had melted away when he met Elayne. "I liked her right away," he says. "She was easy to talk to, and you could tell she was a promoter."

Guindon hoped for a good crowd at the opening. Nevertheless, he was surprised by how big it was. The St. Louis Park police sent a patrolman to direct traffic. People had to park blocks away, then stand in line to get in. Guindon already knew anecdotally that he had an audience, but the fact that hordes of fans turned out to see his work—and buy it—was tangible proof.

He gives Elayne Lindberg much of the credit for the show's success.

"Looking back on it, I'd say she was just what I needed," he says. "She had the energy of a Greek restaurant owner and the heart of a carny. And clearly she was an excellent business woman."

The 1978 LeRoy Neiman show at the gallery made a huge splash—and lots of money. It came about after Elayne's tour of galleries in New York the year before, when she attended an opening of Neiman's work at a downtown gallery. The vibes there were even stiffer than they normally are at such events, because of the odd niche that Neiman occupied in the art world. Commercially he was a major success, but reservations about his bona fides as an artist dogged him. Was there something intrinsically schlocky about brilliantly colored, representational paintings of horse races and football games? Did that weird moustache signal true eccentricity, or was it a publicity stunt? Was he an artist or an illustrator?

Such questions hovered in the air and made for a nervous silence at the opening. People were unwilling to exchange small talk for fear of betraying a forbidden enthusiasm that could open them up to a devastating put-down.

Elayne, oblivious to the awkwardness that suffused

the atmosphere like toxic fog, hauled a Polaroid camera out of her shoulder bag, approached a painting, and clicked the shutter. Instead of a soft, reassuring whir, the mechanism emitted a jarring clatter and began spitting snapshot-sized blanks all over the floor. There was no stopping it.

"Oh my," she said.

The rest of the guests stood frozen in place for a moment, then, hesitantly at first but with an energy that built around the communal chore, began picking up the blanks. Elayne thanked each of them as they bent to their task, and started chatting with such disarming charm that by the time the floor was clean the ice was broken and the party was on. She and Neiman were on first-name terms before the evening ended, and he agreed to do a show at her gallery.

In 1976, the publishing arm of Circle Fine Art Galleries contracted with Norman Rockwell to produce signed, limited-edition lithographs. As soon as Elayne got wind of it, she made arrangements to become a dealer. A show at Elayne Galleries featuring the lithographs was successful, and Elayne began having visions of another show, this one featuring Rockwell paintings and maybe Rockwell himself.

"She was like a dog on a bone once she got that idea in her head," says her daughter. "She said to me, 'Now

Bonnie, you find out if Mr. Rockwell will come.' I said I didn't know how to reach him, but she just called Stockbridge, Massachusetts, information and asked for his phone number."

A short time later, Elayne took a trip to Stockbridge and dropped in on the Rockwells. The artist was too ill to come downstairs and meet her, but his wife was gracious and friendly. She agreed to help arrange a show that would formally open on February 16, 1978—Norman Rockwell's eighty-fourth birthday. Rockwell wouldn't be there because of his health, but the exhibit had his blessings.

By the time the birthday show occurred, Elayne Galleries and the Eleanor Ettinger Gallery in New York had become the two most important venues for Norman Rockwell's work. The affordability of signed, limited-edition Rockwells brought many new clients into Elayne Galleries, some interested in Rockwell as an artist, others to purchase his work as an investment. Elayne's project had succeeded beyond anyone's expectations, and by some measures put her and her gallery near the top of the art-dealing world.

Nevertheless, investigators would have been slackers to overlook her as a suspect. If the theft was an inside job, no one was in a better position than Elayne. For motivation there was a smidgen of insurance and possession of objects that could be monetized in a variety of ways if you knew the right people—which she did. Her acquaintanceship with thieves and fences certainly piqued the FBI's interest, but what really intrigued them was something they found out the day after the theft. She had been directly involved in the sale of what proved to be a fake Renoir to her client, Buddy Verson.

Elayne met Robert "Buddy" Verson in 1976, when her gallery mounted a show featuring the work of the Missouri-born artist Charles Bragg. Verson, then thirty-eight and a resident of Minnetonka, Minnesota, dropped in to view the art because he had received a circular in the mail. He didn't buy anything that day, but he did purchase a Bragg and two Rockwell lithographs soon after. He told Elayne he wanted to hear about future shows. Over the next two years, he spent about $15,000 at the gallery.

"I'd see Buddy at shows," says Gary Lindberg. "He was kind of full of himself, a cocky entrepreneur type, a little too much bluster. I remember him being with a very attractive woman, dark hair, someone you'd notice. Probably not his wife, at least that's how it looked to me. It was something about the way they were together. And she seemed too young."

A few weeks before the Rockwell show, Verson had

approached Elayne with a proposition. As Elayne explained it to investigators, Verson said he had become aware of the availability of a very valuable painting at a bargain price. A Spanish-speaking stewardess who flew for Northwest Airlines had tipped him off. Her name was Sonia (last name unknown, possibly Villarine—in any case, it started with a V).

Verson needed to find out if the Renoir he had been offered was genuine. He enlisted Elayne to authenticate it. He told her that if she agreed, he could arrange to have Sonia V meet her in Miami and take her to see the painting.

On February 8, 1978, Elayne flew to Miami at Verson's expense, carrying $2,000 in cash he had given her and a blank check he had endorsed. Her instructions were to examine the painting and, if she deemed it authentic, to negotiate a purchase price and complete the deal. The sellers were asking $15,000.

Sonia V met Elayne at the Miami airport and drove her to a storage facility where the painting was kept. On the way, they stopped at a motel and picked up a man who said he was the painting's owner. He spoke only Spanish, so Sonia V translated as she wove her way through the midday traffic.

His story—as she told it—was that he had been a Cuban politician of some influence and independent means during the Batista dictatorship. He had invested large sums of money in art, but, sadly, he was forced to leave most of his collection in Cuba after the Castro revolution, from which he barely escaped with his life. He managed to bring the Renoir with him to Florida. It was available for a bargain price due to his straitened circumstances.

As he spoke, they proceeded to the Withers Warehouse in Coral Gables. There, a third individual—a man who simply appeared but never talked about his role in the transaction—handed a painting to Elayne and asked her to identify the artist.

She looked for a few moments at the cube-shaped angles and the peculiar, broken image of a face, and said, "Picasso." The man smiled and nodded approval of her qualifications. The owner took the prize out of a vault for her perusal.

Elayne examined it for almost half an hour, during which she administered a "blue light test" and a "varnish test," before pronouncing it authentic. She placed a collect call to Verson, who told her to go ahead with the deal but to try to beat the price down.

Elayne and the owner negotiated through Sonia V. The other man stood aside, but he must have been listening, because he nodded again when Elayne raised her bid from $8,000 to $10,000 and called it her final offer. The owner agreed, reluctantly it seemed, but he told Elayne that the check she was carrying wouldn't do. The transaction would have to be cash. While she was pondering how to make that happen, the other man reminded the owner that two signatures were required before the Renoir could be released.

"He said the other fellow who had to sign was in Santo Domingo," Elayne told investigators.

Calls were made, arrangements finalized. Verson would fly to Miami the next day with cash to close the deal. As luck would have it, there was a flight due from Santo Domingo at about the same time, so the document could be signed as required.

Meanwhile, another document was prepared, hand-written, stating that either Elayne, Sonia, or Buddy Verson "will pick up the Renoir, original oil at a time when both Rolando [unintelligible—possibly Aherene] and Caesario Concannon are present at Withers Transfer & Storage of Coral Gables inc."

Rolando A is the Cuban. Caesario Concannon is the man who was waiting at the warehouse. A skeptic might wonder why they both have Latin given names and surnames that sound more Irish than anything, but those are the only identifiers that exist for them.

Elayne left Miami the next morning, before Verson and the mystery man from the islands arrived. She

Buddy Verson and his "Renoir"

didn't see the Renoir again until February 13, when Verson brought it into the gallery to put it on display. She told the FBI that she immediately noticed the scratch on the right-hand corner, and she told Verson it was not damaged when she had examined it. He explained that he had been showing it to friends at home, and it must have happened then. He didn't seem concerned about the damage.

Verson and Elayne discussed whether it should be in the upcoming show. Elayne was hesitant because it would clash with the Rockwell theme, but Verson was insistent, and she ultimately agreed that such a valuable work would add to the luster of the event. She decided to hang it in a small room off the main display, and she made Verson promise that he would insure it. He said he would, but he didn't, on the erroneous assumption that the gallery already had insurance on everything that hung there. Three days later the show opened, and the painting was stolen.

The FBI pondered this chain of events, checked their records on the other individuals involved, and concluded that Elayne Lindberg had no role in the theft.

7

THAT LEFT ONE MORE INSIDER, ROBERT "BUDDY" VERSON. After their initial investigations, the FBI assumed that he was the key. Their inquiry centered on whether he was a dupe, a perpetrator, or both.

They couldn't help noticing an eerie similarity between Verson's experience with the fake Renoir and that of a New York–area resident who had been duped by a fake art scam. He had approached the FBI three years earlier, and some parts of the file on that matter are included in the Elayne Galleries file.

A word about FBI files here, because they are crucial sources for the telling of this story. FBI files resemble good literature in two respects. Number one, what is left out is just as important as what is included. The reader has to fill in the blanks. This can be a powerful tool for a good writer of literature, but the FBI carries it to ludicrous extremes. An entire file page may contain only a few words. The rest consists of black stripes, indicating where lines, phrases, and complete paragraphs (you know when a paragraph is gone because the stripe at the bottom is shorter than the ones that precede it) have been "redacted."

That term—*redacted*—is the FBI's, and it was apparently chosen over the more appropriate *deleted* for a reason. *Redact* is a verb meaning "to put into suitable literary form, to revise, to edit." But police reports, court documents, and official records in general are not normally revised and edited. Stories are. In fact, when records and reports are revised and edited, they *become* stories, and therein lies another resemblance between FBI files and good literature: when the FBI responds to a Freedom of Information Act request, they have a story to tell, but it's not necessarily the one you want to hear.

The highly redacted documents concerning the dupe from New York City (name redacted, "A" for the purposes of this summary) reveal that in 1975, he and two partners, "D" and "E," purchased a painting titled "St. Peter," purportedly by the famed seventeenth-century Dutch painter Rembrandt van Rijn. A had been tipped about the availability of the painting by "B aka C," who provided a written appraisal from Rikki's Art Studios, Inc., Miami, valuing the painting at $375,000.

After A and his partners purchased their Rembrandt (price redacted), they stored it in a warehouse in New York City along with two other valuable paintings, one said to be by the Italian artist Michelangelo Merisi da Caravaggio, the other by the Spaniard Diego Velazquez. Both paintings were said to date from the turn of the seventeenth century. According to the file, they had been acquired through someone identified as "B/C" as well.

B/C told A that four paintings—the Velazquez, the Caravaggio, and two Rembrandts titled "St. Peter" and "St. Paul," respectively—had been purchased in Havana in 1953 for $250,000 cash. Initially, he said, the plan had been to carry the paintings, plus $10.5 million in stolen bearer bonds, to Europe for subsequent sale. But that fell through.

A went to the FBI in August 1975, when he became aware that one of his partners—further identified in the file as an officer of the Anthony Abraham Auto Agency in Miami—had removed the Rembrandt and one of the other paintings (it doesn't say which) from the New York warehouse without A's permission.

A gave photos of the missing paintings to the FBI. They were shown to the curator of European art at the Metropolitan Museum, who said both were low-quality fakes. At that point the FBI decided not to open an investigation, but the file does indicate that B/C remained a person of interest. It contains an entry noting that in March 1976, B/C made an appointment with the Sotheby Parke-Bernet Gallery in New York, where he attempted to sell a painting he claimed was by the twentieth-century Austrian Expressionist Oskar Kokoschka. It was immediately spotted as a fake.

The summary of the New York matter appears to be included in the Elayne Galleries file for three reasons: (1) B/C is identified elsewhere in the files as Rolando A, the Cuban who sold Verson the fake Renoir; (2) Rikki's Art Studios, Inc., provided appraisals of both the fake Rembrandt purchased by A and his partners and Verson's fake Renoir; and (3) fake paintings were sold, then stolen, in both cases.

It is easy to deduce what avenues of inquiry the FBI might have pursued, based on the similarities between the two matters. How does Rolando A, a bold con man who is not averse to attempting to peddle a second-rate fake to a prestigious gallery, find more likely victims? Does an attractive, dark-haired young woman named Sonia lure them into the scheme? Is Rikki's Art Studios in on the scam? Is it a coincidence that fakes were stolen after they were sold in both cases, and if not, what could explain that?

Buddy Verson was the link between the two situations, and the FBI gathered information about him at a furious pace for a while, hoping to solve the Minnesota theft plus what they viewed as a New York case worthy of their renewed consideration. They hoped to bring federal charges against the Miami men and anyone who aided in their scheme. The crime would be transporting people, goods, and information via interstate commerce in furtherance of theft and fraud.

Verson, a graduate of St. Paul Central High School in 1955, didn't leave much of an impression on his classmates. The one thing that several of them recall so many years later is that his fair skin and blue eyes belied his Russian-Jewish heritage. According to the yearbook, he played tennis on the Central team and belonged to the Radio Club. He was about five feet ten inches and a little on the pudgy side in high school, more so later in life.

"We never got to know each other very well," says his cousin and classmate Ronald Verson, a Chicago lawyer.

"You know, I remember him but I don't remember anything about him, if that makes any sense. He was a nice guy, I guess I remember that much," says his classmate Howard Abel of Newport Beach, California.

"Blue eyes, right, but I don't recall anything else about him," says another classmate, Butch Salita of St. Paul.

According to other sources, while he was in high school Buddy Verson met a girl from North Dakota at Herzl Camp, a Jewish summer camp in Webster, Wisconsin. They married soon after he graduated. He worked in her family's business in Bismarck after the marriage, but eventually the couple relocated to the Twin Cities area. Verson invested in a wholesale business called Budget Liquors, and in 1972 became partners with a Minneapolitan, the late Robert Bell, in a bar called the "1 & 44" in Shakopee, Minnesota.

"There was a restaurant as well as a bar," says Bell's younger brother, Eddy. "I'm sure of that, because the family celebrated a couple of occasions there. I can kind of see Buddy when I think about it, but I never knew him."

The file refers to Verson as "a bar owner and a wholesale liquor distributor." However, licensing restrictions made it difficult if not impossible to be both in Minnesota. A sense of how Verson handled that problem—or more accurately, took advantage of the opportunities it presented—can be gathered from a memorandum in the file. It concerns some information the FBI received from an agent of the U.S. Bureau of Alcohol, Tobacco and Firearms. The agent said that an inspection of the books at 1 & 44 revealed that "Verson had taken some $100,000 out of the business in an unauthorized fashion" and the co-owner was cooperating "regarding Verson's possible illegal liquor activities."

According to the memo, there were discussions under way between Verson and his partner about liquidating the business and dividing the assets after taking into account the unauthorized withdrawal, which would have left Verson with less than nothing.

There is reference to a "gal friend of Verson's" and "two hit men who did a lot of work for Buddy," one of whom is described as a "large white male." Redactions render that part of the tale more enigmatic than it might be otherwise, but it appears to relate to the pending liquidation.

"There is talk that Buddy may have been into hot items from time to time," according to the memo, and is "also into"—followed by a redaction long enough to cover a multitude of sins.

The FBI file—this memo in particular—supports hearsay about Verson which suggests that by the mid-1970s he was no longer the pleasant but unremarkable young fellow who graduated from Central High School. He had separated from his wife after a long spell of philandering, during which he became notorious for consummating affairs in a dentist's chair in his office. He owned some real estate, including a house in which he allowed young women to live rent free in return for sex, and was rumored to be a fence specializing in high-end items.

Two people who knew about his activities at that time called him "a ball-buster" and "a dangerous man," but another dismissed him as "a wannabe gangster," someone who dabbled in things and consorted with people "he had no business messing around with."

One of those people was Sonia V, the "gal friend" the memo mentions. Her predilections offer a clue about the $100,000 hole Verson dug for himself and the desperate schemes he concocted to get out of it.

Sonia made no secret of her fondness for cocaine, according to Brent Baskfield, vice president of in-flight services for Northwest Airlines while she was a stewardess, nor did she discourage gossip about her connections with gangsters. Baskfield, a sometime client of Elayne Galleries, was a bemused witness to Sonia's flamboyant trajectory through their mutual workplace. When she was off duty, he observed, she took frequent trips to expensive places and wore stylish clothing and jewelry that was unaffordable for someone living on a flight attendant's salary.

"She had kind of an exotic look—dark skin, dark hair," says Baskfield. "Her last name was Spanish-sounding, hard to pronounce. She was very pleasant, but there was always a mysterious aura about her, as if she was way out on the edge and knew things nobody else knew."

Buddy Verson was interviewed twice in connection with the theft, by the FBI and by an insurance adjuster named John Malone. There is a summary of the FBI interview in the Elayne Galleries file. The Malone interview is included in its entirety, with surprisingly few redactions.

On February 23, 1978, Verson told the FBI he had known Sonia for two years and through her was aware of paintings owned by a friend of hers, a Cuban exile and former politician. One in particular, a Renoir oil painting, "was available for immediate purchase." He wasn't much interested at first, because he knew nothing about oil paintings, but the fact that she had "influential friends" in Miami made him curious. She kept talking about it, and earlier that month he had decided to buy it.

He considered keeping it to display at his residence, but an insurance agent advised him that he would have to take pricey security measures if he did, so he contacted Elayne Lindberg and asked her to display it at the gallery, where he assumed it would be insured.

He told the FBI agent that on the morning of February 16, Elayne had called him to say that another painting belonging to Rolando A, this one by an artist named "Dominique," could be purchased for $7,000, and if it was authentic it was worth up to $90,000. Rolando A wanted to sell it in the next two weeks. Verson said he took that under advisement.

That evening he attended the opening of the Rockwell show. Early the next morning he was awakened by a phone call from Elayne informing him that the gallery had been burglarized and his painting had been stolen.

In his interview, he told the FBI agent that the most he could recover from his homeowner's policy was $4,000 and he hoped the gallery's insurance would reimburse him in the amount he paid for the Renoir, $10,000. He said he had no intention of claiming the appraised value of $125,000.

As for the Dominique, he wouldn't be purchasing it because he didn't have the cash and also "because of the unusual circumstances surrounding the purchase and theft of his Renoir oil painting."

When Verson was interviewed by the insurance adjuster, he said that he had been collecting art since 1976 and he owned signed, stone-cut prints and lithographs by Picasso, Bragg, and Calder, as well as Rockwell. He said Sonia was from Miami and her family was acquainted with the owner of the Renoir.

"I know a little history about him," Verson told the adjustor. "He was some kind of Cuban politician in pre-Castro days, and back then they were aware Castro was coming, and there wasn't much they could do about it, and they knew that money would be of no value to them so he converted his money into art works. . . . They had trouble getting the paintings out of the country. This painting [the Renoir] was gotten out through the Japanese embassy."

He explained that the second signatory for the sale of the Renoir, the man from Santo Domingo, had some connection to the Japanese embassy there. He was "a kid," but later in the interview Verson described him as "about fifty" and "a medical student."

Malone didn't follow up on those contradictions. He did ask if it struck Verson as peculiar that a painting appraised at $125,000 could be purchased for $10,000.

"You betcha!" Verson replied (exclamation point courtesy of the FBI). "That's why I flew Elayne down to authenticate it."

He went on to explain that the difference between fine art and Disney cartoons was lost on him. He preferred his young son's finger paintings.

8

As soon as she unloaded the fake Renoir, Sonia began pestering Elayne and Verson about another deal that she could midwife. According to her, two more paintings were available. One was the work of the nineteenth-century French painter Jean-Baptiste Corot. The other was by an artist identified—on the affidavit establishing provenance and ownership (still Spain 1946, but Cuba 1957 this time)—as "Jean-Auguste Dominique."

It would take $14,000 to gain possession of the paintings, and that would be in the nature of a down payment. Profit from their resale would be split with the sellers in Miami. Verson wanted to go ahead with it, but plans were put on hold because of the theft and the hard feelings that flared up between Verson and Elayne, based on his mistaken assumption that every piece in the show had been insured by the gallery.

Verson's initial reaction when Elayne Lindberg told him about the theft of his Renoir, as quoted in the file, was, "worse things could happen." Then he discovered that the paintings on consignment were not insured.

"My mom had told Buddy in no uncertain terms that he had to insure his own painting," says Bonnie, "but he never did, and he was angry when he found out we hadn't either. It didn't last long, though. He needed her to complete the other deal."

It was during this brief estrangement—it lasted less than a week—that Elayne told investigators about her Miami experience and the potential second trip there to buy more art. On March 2 the FBI enlisted her help in a sting operation.

Although Elayne was crucial to the scheme the FBI hatched, she was kept in the dark about several things. The file references an FBI agent with an art background who would accompany her to Miami. The agent noted that Corot is "one of the most highly faked artists," but Elayne didn't need to know that, nor did she need to know about the agent's expertise. Her opinion about the paintings' authenticity was to be "solely for the investigative assistance of the bureau." In other words, she would offer her evaluation as one episode in a tightly scripted performance, staged so that "agent can meet [redacted] observe his operation and greatly assist in determining scope of his activities."

The file notes that Rolando A already appeared to

be in violation of Title 18, USC, section 2314, in connection with the sale of the fake Renoir, and that records indicate that he had been involved in "questionable art sales since at least 1975."

The moment Verson's attitude about the insurance softened, Sonia urged him to get the money together quickly and purchase the paintings. The deal he arranged was structured as a partnership between himself and a contractor named Robert Johnstone. They agreed to put up $7,000 each to buy the two paintings.

On March 2, Verson gave Elayne $7,000 cash and a personal check made out to her from Johnstone for the same amount. The next day, she and the special agent flew to Miami.

"The agent told Mom to introduce him as her nephew, a wealthy industrialist who was interested in acquiring some art," says Bonnie. "I think they made that up on the plane. The whole thing was put together quickly, because Sonia wanted the deal to move fast."

They arrived in midafternoon and were met at the airport by Rolando A and Caesario Concannon. Sonia had arranged for the viewing of the paintings to take place at her parents' home. She was supposed to be at the airport, too, but her flight had been delayed, so they had to wait.

When she finally arrived hours later, she was her

usual vivacious self. She flirted with the wealthy young industrialist and uttered asides in Spanish, including one in which she referred to Elayne as "La Maestra." She said she could hardly wait to see the paintings. She displayed her crossed fingers and said she was praying to Jesus, Mary, and the Heavenly Father, the whole trinity, that they were authentic.

Concannon said he would rent a car, pick up the paintings at the Japanese embassy, and meet them at Sonia's family's home. Rolando A said everyone else could ride in his car, which was parked at the airport. As they parted company, a second FBI man who had been lurking nearby began shadowing Concannon. The agent kept a surveillance log of what he observed over the next few hours.

Elayne, Rolando A, Sonia, and the undercover agent left in Rolando A's car. Sonia gave directions to her parents' house in English. Rolando A followed the directions unerringly, but when the undercover agent asked a question about other paintings that might be available, Sonia had to translate.

"Mas tarde," was Rolando A's reply.

"He says we can talk about it later," said Sonia.

Meanwhile, Concannon had rented a car and left the airport, but he didn't go to the Japanese embassy. According to the surveillance log, he drove to "Rikki

Galleries," 2256 Coral Way, in Coral Gables, and let himself in the back way.

While he was inside, a second car, a Ford station wagon, pulled up in front. The driver moved over to the passenger side and waited. Concannon emerged about fifteen minutes later with "a large object covered with wrapping paper." He placed it in the back seat of the station wagon and drove that vehicle to Sonia's family's residence, a short distance away.

Concannon took the package inside and remained there for about an hour. The other man stayed in the car the whole time.

The home was small and crowded. Sonia's mother, father, sister, her sister's boyfriend, and their child were all there when Rolando A and his passengers arrived. Concannon walked in a few minutes later, and everyone gathered in the living room to view the paintings. He carefully unwrapped the package. There were gasps as he revealed the masterpieces.

The painting by "Jean-Auguste Dominique" was a portrait of a woman wearing an elaborately wound turban, roughly five feet by three feet. She held a scroll of music, and the bow of a cello could be seen resting against her shoulder. The Corot, a landscape with three female figures dancing a ring around a tree, was quite a bit smaller, about two feet by one and a half feet.

The room hushed for the appraisal. Elayne asked if the lights could be turned out so she could examine the painting under a black light she had brought along, a test that sometimes reveals clues about an object's age and detects repairs that are invisible to the naked eye.

When that test was finished, she asked for the lights again and removed the Dominique from its frame to examine the back-lining.

"I think they're both authentic," she announced.

Rolando A beamed as she proceeded to estimate their value—$135,000 for the Dominique, $125,000 for the Corot—but the best part, she said, was that even if they were not authentic, they were so old, and of such high quality, that they would still be worth in the neighborhood of $30,000 each, maybe more.

Elayne's nephew said that if there were any other paintings like that lying around, he would like to take a look at them. Sonia translated for Rolando, who nodded enthusiastically, and said there were four more stashed at the Japanese embassy. Sonia gave Elayne's nephew her phone number and said she could act as a go-between in any deal he wanted to make.

A deal for the Corot and the Dominique was quickly struck. Storage charges of $7,000 for each painting, payable to the Japanese embassy, would be covered by the $14,000 Elayne brought with her. The paintings would then become the property of Verson and John-stone (who had agreed to take one each as their share), but they would be displayed for sale at Elayne Galleries, priced in the neighborhood of her assessments. When they were sold, the partners would take their $7,000 off the top, Elayne would take her fee, and the rest would be split fifty-fifty between Rolando and the partners.

Elayne gave Rolando $7,000 cash for the Corot and arranged for Sonia to hand-carry the painting to Min-neapolis on a Northwest flight the next day. She signed the check that Verson's partner had given her. Sonia was instructed to cash it early the next morning. If that transaction went smoothly, she would bring the Domi-nique to Minneapolis as well.

Before Elayne left, she took photos of the paintings. She explained that as a precaution she wanted to send them to a friend in France for a second opinion.

There are only hints and snippets about what hap-pened over the next few weeks. What's certain is that both paintings made it back to Minneapolis. Verson took possession of the Corot, and Johnstone got the Jean-Auguste Dominique.

The photos of the Corot and the Dominique were turned over to the FBI. There is a file entry that con-sists of instructions to "determine if enclosed photo-graph would assist in resolving if 'Corot' is stolen, fake, or if New York has determined that future undercover contacts by New York agent knowledgeable in painting field should be made with Miami regarding activities of [redacted—undoubtedly Sonia] in Minnesota."

Sonia showed up at the gallery with a Northwest Airlines pilot and his wife on March 28. Sonia told Elayne that she had spoken to Elayne's nephew (the undercover agent) about buying a painting by the Dutch Renaissance artist Gerard van Honthorst that was available in Miami. He had promised to get back to her. She asked Elayne to tell him that she needed to hear from him soon, because the pilot was interested in buying it, too.

At that point everything was working to perfection for the FBI. They had witnessed an act of fraud. The acts that tied it to interstate commerce had occurred. They had a credible entry into an organized crime ring and reason to believe it would result in a sale to an undercover agent. They had locales to survey, Rikki's Art Studios and maybe Sonia's family's home, in hopes of walking the scheme back deeper into the Miami mob. Then it all fell apart.

An entry dated April 7, 1978, says that Elayne had informed someone (name redacted, undoubtedly Sonia) that she had heard from her friend in France, and there was no way to tell if the Corot was real or fake based on the photo. As for the Dominique, there would be a delay while some research on the artist himself took place. (Redacted) was said to be "very mad" when she got that news.

Elayne and Sonia spoke heatedly several times about the inconclusive appraisal, and in the course of one of those discussions Elayne blew her cover.

According to a memorandum dated May 22, 1978, "As a result of Elayne Lindberg's revealing to [redacted] presence of Miami FBI during negotiations with [redacted] and [redacted] for paintings purchased by Lindberg, it is felt by Miami that both [redacted] and [redacted] would be skeptical and aware of unknown parties introduced to them by Lindberg in the future.— Since no further leads are outstanding in the Miami area, and no indication of feasible present undercover purchases, this case is being considered RUC."

RUC means "referred upon completion" and is sometimes rendered as "referred upon completion to office of origin." In this case, it meant the big fish had gotten away. Miami and New York were no longer interested. It was up to the staff at the office of origin, Minneapolis, whether they wanted to devote resources to the search for the genuine Rockwells (subsequent events suggest they did not), but the case of the fake master works by Rembrandt, Caravaggio, Jean-Auguste Dominique, et al., was officially moribund.

Too bad. The elements in play and the characters involved promised a bizarre tale, with a number of possible twists. As it is, there are a few principals identified in the files, people with firsthand knowledge can name a few more, and some clues exist about who the others might be. The rest consists of filling in the blanks.

Dark-eyed Sonia, with her cocaine, her gangster friends, and her mysterious aura, is the most intriguing person among those whose identity is known, but at this point in the story she floats off like a bubble and pops. It turns out that even the name by which she's remembered might be wrong.

"Villarine" is an anglicized form of what Bonnie Lindberg and Brent Baskfield, who knew her and dealt with her, can agree on when they consult their memories. According to her scrawled signature on a notarized document prepared in connection with the sale of the fake Renoir (spelled "Renua"), dated March 2, 1978, her name was actually Maria Elena *something*—possibly Villarin, but it looks more like Villorreni, or maybe even Villoran, a common name in Miami.

According to a story that can't be verified but is too good to ignore, she didn't exactly make a secret of her identity, but when she introduced herself she was in the habit of running her two given names and her surname together into one long phoneme à la español, complete with rolling Rs and trilled Ls, thus rendering it unintelligible to most people. When they looked puzzled, she would say, "Oh, just call me Sonia." It was one of the little enigmas she thrived on.

"Everything she got into was questionable," says Baskfield. "I don't know about the fake paintings, but she certainly smuggled cocaine. She was caught. I wasn't supervising her at the time, but the person who was received a call one day, and was told that Sonia wouldn't be available for work because she was in jail. They'd patted her down when she got off an international flight in Miami and found cocaine. I don't recall exactly when that happened, but it was a while after the paintings were stolen from Elayne's. It was common knowledge around Northwest that she'd gone to prison for it. Then a few years later I heard she was run over by a car and killed."

Maybe, but no known version of her name appears in the Social Security death register.

Buddy Verson was a complicated character. Apparently he grew tired of being the blue-eyed boy everybody liked but nobody remembered, so he dreamed up a new version of himself. It didn't end well, but at least he had the chutzpah to live the dream for a while. You can sense a quick mind at work in his banter with the insurance adjuster. That dentist's chair is a nice touch. Unfortunately, his story is over before the case was RUC. On March 29, 1978, he died of a heart attack while running around the track at an athletic club on the 494 strip. He was forty years old.

The note in the FBI file about his death states that the Corot, which had been hanging in his home, was now in possession of (redacted). According to Bonnie, he consigned it to Elayne Galleries for sale before he died.

Conjecture about the other painting's origins, and its niche in art history, touches on issues central to the kind of aesthetic questions that arise when people buy art or simply look at it. It is a pleasing and nicely executed work, created as a copy of another painting, either as an exercise in draftsmanship or in pursuit of some idealized form of beauty. It became a fake only because it fell into the hands of frauds, who claimed it was painted by "Jean-Auguste Dominique."

Dominique is such an excellent name for an artist that there are always several around. The landscape painter John Augustus Dominique (1893–1994) might be the best known at present, but we also have the wildlife artist Dominique Salm; Dominique Reneé, a self-styled "Nail Artist and Designer"; and the French artist Dominique Amendola, who paints figures and spiritual fine art. In the long history of European art, there is no record of anyone named "Jean-Auguste

Dominique." Certainly no one by that name has ever created a masterpiece.

It appears that Rolando A and his confederate, Caesario Concannon, the central figures in an organized crime ring that sold knockoffs of masterpieces for years, didn't bother finding out who was supposed to have painted that particular fake. They were used to dealing with people who couldn't tell the difference between an Impressionist landscape and a Disney cartoon.

Elayne Lindberg was playing a role when she assessed the painting. Whether she knew she was authenticating the work of an artist who never existed is unclear.

The unnamed expert who examined the photo for the FBI referred to it at first as a "purported Dominique," but the next reference in the file speculates that it might be a knockoff of a painting by the Italian artist Guido Reni (1575–1642). Eventually the FBI identified it as a "copy of a work hanging in a Roman museum, painted by the French neoclassicist Jean-Auguste Dominique Ingres."

It is unclear whether this ambiguously stated entry means that the expert believed that Ingres (1780–1867), an acknowledged master, painted the original that hangs in the unnamed Roman museum or that Ingres executed a copy of someone else's work that was hanging there.

If it were the latter, the painting would be worth a small fortune, but the copy is unsigned and there is no historical basis for attributing it to Ingres other than the fact that he lived in Rome for many years. As for the former, there is no painting by Ingres in Rome or anywhere else that looks even vaguely like the "purported Dominique," although it does bear one stylistic quirk associated with him.

Ingres moved to Rome in 1806. It marked the beginning of an odd period in his life. He was twenty-six, and his work was about to show at the Paris Salon. He seemed to be on the verge of major success, but the reception his paintings received in Paris was negative, and he remained in self-imposed exile in Italy for the next twenty years, first in Rome, then in Bologna. During that time he received very few commissions for the kind of grand-scale, neoclassical works that were his natural bent. He learned how to do portraits grudgingly, for money, and probably devoted a fair amount of time to studying notable examples of portraiture at local galleries. For a while he relied on the sale of small pencil portraits of tourists to make a living. He produced hundreds of them.

The true identity of the portrait attributed to "Jean-Auguste Dominique" was up in the air when it arrived in Minneapolis, but very soon after, in April 1978,

Elayne wrote a noted art critic in New York about it and enclosed some photos. He told her he'd need to examine the painting itself to draw any real conclusions, but not to get her hopes up about its value.

"Bob Johnstone was pretty disappointed," says Bonnie. "He asked us to sell it for him."

It hung in Elayne Galleries until November 1996, when Brent Baskfield purchased it. "I think we paid in the neighborhood of $2,500," he says.

Baskfield was curious about its history and made some inquiries. First he asked Thomas Blanck of St. Paul, a specialist in historical architecture and restoration, to determine its age. Blanck determined that it was painted between 1800 and 1850. Baskfield then sent photos to Robert Rosenblum, an art critic and curator at the Solomon R. Guggenheim Museum in New York.

In a letter dated February 4, 1997, Rosenblum writes: "Your painting is a copy of a very famous painting by Domenichino (A Sibyl) in Rome, hanging in the Galleria Borghese. It was copied dozens, or more likely, hundreds of times. Unless there is some documentary evidence (a genuine signature, an important history of ownership, etc.), I cannot imagine how anybody could determine who made the copy. Word of mouth tradition that it is by Ingres or a student of Ingres hardly holds any weight in the court of art history."

Domenico Zampieri, called "Domenichino" because of his diminutive stature, was a much-loved seventeenth-century Italian painter. A native of Bologna, he moved to Rome as a student and achieved his reputation there. He executed four paintings called "Sibyls" (women with oracular powers) during his career. The best known is "The Cumaean Sibyl," owned by the Capitoline Museums in Rome.

Domenichino's Sibyls are portraits of young women with images relating to music prominent in the com-

Florence and Brent Baskfield with their "Dominique"

The copy of Domenichino's sibyl hanging at the home of Brent and Florence Baskfield

positions—allusions to the legend that sibyls sang their prophecies to the accompaniment of musical instruments. They are considered to be examples of seventeenth-century portraiture at its best.

No one knows if Ingres copied one (or more) of them, but there were a few things that might have interested him about Domenichino and his Sibyls. Ingres had a special interest in music. The cello-like bow (it's actually a viola da gamba) in the background of Baskfield's copy would certainly have caught his eye. Cellos became something of an obsession for Ingres. He spent quite a bit of time in his long career looking at nude women from various angles, and at some point it occurred to him that seated, and viewed from the rear, a woman's body is shaped like a cello. "La Grande Odalisque," painted in 1814 and housed at the Louvre Museum in Paris, is a good example of how he handled that insight artistically.

In 1924, the Dadaist Man Ray, an admirer of Ingres, made the resemblance explicit by painting the filigreed holes of a cello on a model's bare back and photographing her from the rear. He called the image "Le Violon d'Ingres," a double entendre. *Violon d'Ingres* is a French slang expression, meaning an activity "other than that for which one is well known, or at which one excels." It derives from the fact that after he moved back to Paris,

Ingres became notorious for an idiosyncrasy. Visitors to his studio were routinely subjected to an impromptu concert on the violin, which he played passionately but badly. Legend has it he lost a lot of sales that way.

Ingres may have recognized a kindred soul in Domenichino, who was known as a lover of music and an inventor of musical instruments as well as a painter. It's quite a stretch to say that he copied Domenichino's Sibyl, but the Italian artist would have been flattered if he did.

Domenichino subscribed to the aesthetic theory of Imitation, which posits that ideal beauty in art is attained through the study and imitation of earlier art. His pursuit of the ideal got him embroiled in a famous controversy, in which he was accused of copying a painting by his teacher and claiming it as his own. He was defended vigorously by his fellow artists and remained outspoken in his belief that copying a work of art is a creative process—but only if the goal is to surpass the model.

9

THE FILE GOES INTO DETAIL ABOUT HOW THE FBI THOUGHT
Verson fit into the pattern of events that includes the
theft at Elayne Galleries. It comes in the form of the ra-
tionale for the sting. After summarizing the plan to buy
the two additional paintings, it states:

> Minneapolis investigation to date has determined
> there is high probability Renoir is a fake which may be
> substantiated by previous activities of [redacted]. Min-
> neapolis feels burglary may well have been staged to
> retrieve fake Renoir, Rockwells being taken as added
> profit to burglars for the following reasons:
>
> 1) The 3 individuals who allegedly cased the gallery,
> one of whom, [redaction, medium length, four or five
> words], made a point to congregate in the area of the
> Renoir which was away from the main gallery area.
> This indicates the Renoir was likely the primary target
> of the theft.

2) There is a high probability the Renoir is a fake and of virtually no value.

3) Due to organized crime connections [redacted] and [redacted] it is feasible to assume [redacted] could have been contacted to retrieve the Renoir by organized crime types.

4) [Redacted] has been contacted by organized crime element for "contract" work in past.

5) If the above is the case, [redacted] would have ready outlet to fence Rockwells in addition to having easy access to returning fake Renoir to [redacted].

6) Minneapolis has determined [long redaction, maybe ten words] to theft which may indicate *his* [italics added] purpose of travel was to dispose of painting or paintings.

7) It is logical to assume [redacted] is out to defraud Verson and other buyer due to past activities [redacted] as well as the fact he is attempting to "move" them for additional $14,000 through arrangement set forth above.

8) In order to "move" Verson and other buyer for the $14,000 it would be essential to have spurious painting out of the way to preclude discovery of the scheme.

If this was a lawyer show on television, now would be the time when the investigator has to explain all those modal verbs: What do you mean, "may indicate"? Why is it "feasible to assume"? How likely are all these likelihoods? How probable are the probabilities?

The case being made, however conditionally, is for the Verson-as-dupe scenario, with mobsters from Miami hiring expert thieves to retrieve a fake painting. The thieves' cut is possession of the Rockwells. It is as likely as any of the other scenarios, of which there are many. In one, Verson is a wannabe gangster who told some real gangsters about an opportunity, which they checked out more or less on a whim and found to their liking. In another, Verson is a ball-busting fence going for the money several ways at once, buying fake art and trying to sell it, arranging the theft of genuine art and overseeing its subsequent sale.

Variations on each of those scenarios make Sonia the central figure, which seems more likely. She had the necessary insider's knowledge through Verson and the established connection with the Miami mob.

What all the postulated scenarios have in common is the names of certain people and either knowledge of or speculation about their activities. The names of the alleged perpetrators and some of their activities are redacted in the official version.

For example, scenario #6 above uses the conclusive-sounding verb "determined" to describe what has been learned about "*his*" purpose of travel. "He," according to numerous other entries in the file, is a man who traveled from Chicago to Minneapolis shortly before the theft. He had worked on a contract basis for organized crime in the past (#4), and it is feasible to assume he was contacted by Rolando A and his confederate to retrieve the Renoir (#3).

The names of that man and three well-known Twin Cities characters—two of them with organized crime ties—are consistently mentioned in the hearsay, speculation, and alleged firsthand information about the theft at Elayne Galleries.

An informant, reached through a former Hennepin County attorney, claims to have firsthand knowledge.

"Sure I know who stole the paintings," he says. "So did the cops and the FBI, but they didn't have enough evidence to charge anybody." He named four perpetrators, among them the thief from Chicago.

There are many allusions to individuals who seem to be those four in the FBI files (#1 above, for example), and they are the central characters in every scenario, on or off the record, that has been posed to explain it. Their descriptions, as freshly recollected by Russ and Elayne Lindberg plus other witnesses who were working at the gallery, appear several times in the files. Public documents concerning other matters in which they were involved indicate that they are logical suspects.

In 1981, one of them was facing trial for another

matter. If convicted, his penalty was likely to be severe. Court documents state that he contacted the FBI and offered to return all the stolen paintings if that would result in a favorable plea bargain, but no deal was made. Those charges were ultimately dropped because a key witness refused to testify.

Three of the four are still living, and in deference to the laws of libel and defamation cannot be named, even though the statute of limitations has run out on the theft.

Kent Anderson passed away in 2007, at the age of seventy-two. According to his obituary, he was a resident of Ham Lake, Minnesota, when he died.

"Kent was there for the job, but mainly he was a fence," says the informant. He supposedly had first rights to sell the stolen art, but he wasn't able to do so.

Carol Hines of Hopkins, Minnesota, remembers Anderson fondly. He worked with Hines's late husband in the commercial photography business in the 1960s, and they saw him occasionally over the years.

"Kent was a charming, good-looking guy back when I knew him," says Hines. "He was six feet tall or so, had reddish-blond hair. Alligator shoes? Maybe. He could be a sharp dresser when he wasn't down and out. He was one of the funniest people I ever knew—funnier than his brother Louie, in my opinion, but in a different way. I guess that whole family developed a sense of humor in order to survive. Kent just idolized the comedian Jonathan Winters, could mimic him perfectly. You'd laugh so hard it hurt when he was doing his Jonathan Winters shtick. He was smart, good-natured, but—how should I put it—out on the edge. I never knew him to be involved in anything illegal, and I can't imagine him harming anybody, but I guess I wouldn't be real surprised to find out that he took part in a theft. He was the kind of guy who'd fit in any slot, if you know what I mean, and he was up against it many times."

Keith Harstad, a Minneapolis lawyer and developer, recalls Anderson as a guy who always wanted to have fun and raise hell, sometimes at other people's expense.

"He was willing to try anything," Harstad says. "I liked Kent, but was he a solid citizen? No, he wasn't."

Hines doesn't remember Anderson being scarred up or having wires on his teeth, but their contacts were sporadic enough so she could have missed that. She recalls him being "one of Bill Cooley's guys." Cooley, the former mayor of Minnetonka, took pleasure in hiring rogues and ne'er-do-wells who were down on their luck to work at his west suburban dog pound. He kept them on the payroll until they got on their feet again, mostly because he liked to listen to their stories.

"I'm pretty sure Kent had a job as a dogcatcher out at Bill's for a while," says Hines.

A contact between an informer who talked to the FBI about the theft and one of the perpetrators he fingered occurred at Cooley's kennel. There is reference in the files to surveillance that took place there as well.

10

"I GOT A CALL ABOUT TWO YEARS AFTER THE THEFT AT Elayne Galleries," says Minneapolis attorney Joe Friedberg. "The guy wouldn't identify himself or say where he was calling from, but he asked if I was willing to negotiate with the insurers for the return of that art work. The conversation was such that if I didn't do this, he was going to destroy it. I said, 'I don't know if I can. Call back.'"

Friedberg asked the State Professional Responsibility Board if it was ethical to do what the caller proposed. "I told them that the art might be destroyed if someone didn't act," he says.

The board had no position on whether negotiating for the art was ethical but told Friedberg that there had been a case in Ohio where a lawyer had done exactly what he was asked to do and was subsequently convicted of a felony.

"I passed," says Friedberg.

A few weeks later he bumped into Dick Anderson, an FBI agent, at the Berman Buckskin store in Minneapolis. "I'd see him around quite a bit. He was the head of organized crime investigations here, so he had plenty of time on his hands. He asked me, 'Joe, you know anything about the theft at Elayne's?' I told him about the call, but he'd already heard. He must've had a source over at the Board of Professional Responsibility."

That chance encounter and the casual question it elicited were typical of the FBI's efforts at that point. They had begun with several good suspects, but things hadn't panned out, and two years after the paintings were stolen, the investigation was inactive.

Friedberg had another tangential connection to the theft. Minneapolis was home to several master thieves in the 1970s, among them the late Jerrold Conaway. "Jerry was a client of mine. I knew him well," says Friedberg. "He was a very interesting guy, one of a kind."

What made him unique, according to Friedberg, was that he was a sophisticated thief who also had a strong conventional work ethic. Conaway was employed as an asbestos worker on and off for most of his life, which was certainly prolonged by his avocation. He wasn't inhaling asbestos fibers during the time it took to plan and pull off thefts—or while he did several stretches in prison. He died of mesothelioma in 1993, at the age of seventy-six.

"Jerry was also a very accomplished gambling cheat," says Friedberg. "He once got into a crap game at a VFW in St. Paul, and he had what's called an 'arm' on him, which is a die up the sleeve. So it was his turn, he throws, and oops—three dice come out on the table. He knew the jig was up, but before they grabbed him, he said, 'Well then, I guess my point is 18.' They didn't think it was funny. They broke both his arms, and kicked him around some too, put him in the hospital for a while. He told me that in his opinion, he deserved it."

Friedberg defended Conaway in the late 1970s, when Conaway was arrested due to a fluky set of circumstances that began when he took his car into a dealership for repairs. He was given the use of a loaner that had been stolen and recovered several weeks before, but the police had neglected to take it off their hot-car list. A cop spotted the car, pulled it over, and recognized Conaway. The officer ordered him to open the trunk and found it full of merchandise that still had price tags. On the strength of that, a search warrant was issued for Conaway's home, where burglary tools were discovered.

"We tried to get the whole thing quashed because the car wasn't stolen, but the judge ruled that it was an honest mistake on the part of the police," says Friedberg, "so I represented him when he stood trial for possession of stolen merchandise and possession of burglary tools. It was kind of a treat having him for [a] client."

One of the first items entered into evidence was an electrical device taken from Conaway's home that could be magnetically attached to metal. The prosecutor called it a burglary tool.

"Jerry leaned over and said, 'Bullshit, it's a robbery tool, not a burglary tool, and I can show the jury how it's used,'" says Friedberg. "He told me that you follow a jewelry salesman on his route, and when he's inside a store you get under the hood of his car, and you put that thing on the distributor. There is another part to the device that you keep in your car, and you follow the salesman out in the country, push a button in your car, and it disconnects his distributor. Then his car stops and you rob him. So I asked him if he really wanted to testify to that, and he said, 'Sure, I'm charged with possession of burglary tools. There is no such crime as possession of robbery tools.' I told him to go ahead and testify. The jury loved him."

According to Friedberg, Conaway had just returned from Las Vegas when he was arrested in the loaner car. He had been subpoenaed to appear before a grand jury that was investigating the activities of Tony "The Ant" Spillotro, a Chicago mobster who ruled the roost in Vegas from 1971 until he was murdered in 1986.

Spillotro reportedly reached out to the best thieves in the country for guidance in the process of putting together a rogue gang ("the Hole in the Wall Gang") and planning a high-end burglary spree that earned him the wrath of more conservative mobsters, who wanted him to stick to skimming casino revenues. It was their displeasure that cost Spillotro his life.

"Jerry had been referred to me for advice on how to handle that grand jury appearance," says Friedberg. "He told me, 'I'm not answering any questions about Tony Spillotro, no way,' so I advised him to take the fifth. I guess what happened is, they gave him immunity and he still wouldn't answer, so he did a little jail time."

According to the Minneapolis informant, Conaway had a role in planning the theft from Elayne Galleries but did not participate in the actual heist. "He was more like a—what would you call it—a consultant," he says.

"To my knowledge, he wasn't involved at all," says Friedberg.

11

THE MINNEAPOLIS INFORMANT IS A PROPONENT OF THE
Verson-as-wannabe-gangster theory. He claims that
Verson paid for his indiscretions with his life.

According to him, Verson liked hanging around with
tough guys, and he told some well-known Minneapolis criminals about the opportunity at Elayne Galleries.
Verson wanted a cut of whatever profits were realized;
he said that he would be shielded from suspicion because his painting, which he thought was authentic,
was not insured. Thus, he would be seen to have suf-
fered a major loss as a result of the theft.

"The guys he talked to blew him off," says the informant. "They kind of laughed about it, because they
didn't take him seriously. Then they went out there just
for the hell of it, and took a look at that place, the gallery, and said, 'Hey, it's for real.'"

Verson got his cut, says the informant, but his confederates became worried that he was getting shaky when the FBI came after him.

In January 1980, the contractor who had made Elayne Galleries "theft proof" came into the gallery looking for a loan. In the course of a rambling conversation, he revealed that he knew Buddy Verson and then claimed that the mob had used drugs to murder Verson.

The implication was that Verson had shared with the thieves crucial information about the security system that he learned from the contractor, thus enabling them to enter the gallery. But according to the informant, the perpetrators were skilled enough that they didn't need anybody's help breaking in. It sounded like he knew a thing or two about security systems himself.

"There were only a few guys around who could turn alarms off, pick locks, do that kind of stuff," he says. "The police said the lock out there was punched, but it was pulled, it wasn't punched. Back then you had the Ace pick, or the UL pick, or else you just took an ohm meter, clipped it on to see how many ohms were running through, and dialed up the same amount of ohms. Then you could cut the wire, and bypass the system."

Verson's death certificate says he died of a heart attack. No autopsy was performed. Elayne told the FBI about her conversation with the contractor, and they followed one of the men the informant named for a few days immediately afterward. They also contacted the contractor and made a note that he was in a position to develop further information which could very possibly lead to recovery of the paintings. There is no mention of a possible murder.

It makes a better story if Verson was murdered, but his ex-wife, who refused to talk about him in any detail otherwise, said he had a history of heart trouble.

The real problem with the Verson-as-perpetrator scenario, and anything that flows from it, is that it rests on the assumption that he knew his painting wasn't insured. But if that was his story, he forgot to stick to it. He told the FBI that he thought it was insured. According to Bonnie Lindberg, he was visibly disturbed when he found out it wasn't.

"I'm certain he was under the impression we had insurance," says Bonnie. "That second trip to Miami almost didn't happen because he was so mad when he found out it wasn't."

The case of the theft from Elayne Galleries remains unsolved; therefore no explanation can be entirely discounted. But the scenario the FBI proposes is the most likely one. Verson had been duped once; the robbery was part of a scheme to dupe him again, and it worked. He died of natural causes a short time later.

In August 1978, Home Insurance Company paid Elayne Galleries $34,500 for the loss of "The Date Paintings" ($35,000 minus a $500 deductible) and, per the rider on the gallery's policy, paid Brown & Bigelow $89,500 for its four Rockwell paintings (same deductible). The insurer then became the lawful owner of the paintings.

The payoff agreement between Brown & Bigelow and Home Insurance contemplates the possibility of later recovery. It values each individual painting for that purpose. For example, "The Spirit of 1976" is valued at $30,812, which is the price Brown & Bigelow would have to pay Home Insurance if it wanted the painting back. The total for the four paintings equals the $90,000 payout minus the deductible.

The agreement includes this language: "If any reward for the recovery of the property shall be offered, both Brown & Bigelow and Home Insurance Company shall agree in writing to the terms and conditions thereof and the cost thereof shall be borne by both parties jointly."

12

THE TIPSTER WHO HAD FINGERED AN UNDERWORLD FIG-
ure for the Minneapolis police and the FBI three weeks
following the theft practically made a pest of himself
thereafter. He contacted the FBI many times six months
later, named the perpetrators again, and said he didn't
know whether the paintings were still in Minneapolis
or had been fenced elsewhere.

A memorandum dated October 24, 1980, says the
tipster had "continually advised that [redacted] was
responsible for captioned theft." The most interesting
thing about that particular memo is that it is included
as part of the information the FBI developed after
Elayne Lindberg told them of her conversation with
the contractor. He appears to be the tipster who kept
on tipping.

The files indicate that he merely confirmed what
the FBI already knew about the theft, but his periodic

reminders might have prodded them to make life un-comfortable for at least one of the perpetrators.

In 1983, the tipster contacted a retired FBI agent and claimed he could recover the paintings in return for a reward. Elayne told the former agent that there was a $5,000 reward being offered by Home Insurance. She said the company might even go as high as $10,000, if the paintings were in good condition. The former agent said the lower figure was probably plenty and he would stay in contact. Nothing came of it.

In June 1984, correspondence addressed to the Minneapolis office from an agent in the field suggests "reopening" the case because the tipster had new information. He claimed that one of the men he fingered was now in possession of the paintings. The note ends with a caution: "This case should not be discussed on Bureau radio frequencies because it is known that [redacted] has Bureau radio monitored."

Nothing came of that either, but a year later, in the spring of 1985, the thief who allegedly possessed the paintings was under intense surveillance by the FBI. His phone was tapped, and he was being tailed. He was feeling the heat and making plans to relocate.

He phoned Elayne Lindberg and made a proposal. He would return all the stolen paintings if both the U.S. attorney and the Hennepin County attorney would agree not to prosecute. A preliminary meeting was scheduled between Elayne, the perpetrator, and his lawyer, but the perpetrator never showed up.

By August 1985, that same perpetrator was living in Detroit and negotiating through an attorney to set up a deal between himself, the FBI, and Home Insurance Company. By then he wanted immunity plus a cash reward. The FBI was eager to make the deal. They seem to have persuaded the prosecutors to go along, but there were still many stumbling blocks. Each party to the potential arrangement had a separate agenda, even the ones that appeared to be acting in concert.

All of the paintings, seven Rockwells and the fake Renoir, were subject to the negotiation, but Brown & Bigelow cared only about its four paintings (if those), and the insurer had a monetary interest only in those four plus the two that belonged to the gallery. Per the payout agreement, Brown & Bigelow and the insurer had to agree to any arrangement that was made and had to split the cost of a reward.

According to the file, the perpetrator's attorney estimated the value of all the paintings at that point to be $1,115,000. "Similar paintings by Rockwell," said the attorney, "have been sold in the open market for prices in excess of $100,000, a marked increase due to the death of Rockwell since the theft of these paintings."

The value of Rockwell's paintings had spiked after his death, but not as much as the attorney claimed. Even if it had, simple arithmetic indicates that for negotiation purposes the fake Renoir, in which neither the insurer nor Brown & Bigelow had any interest, was being valued as highly as the Rockwell paintings. Maybe higher.

Home Insurance was represented by Greg Smith, now an insurance attorney in New York. "I don't recall being told that the Renoir was a fake," he says. He can't be sure whether his client was aware or not.

It seems likely that the FBI wanted a key piece of evidence and jumped at the chance to have Home Insurance and Brown & Bigelow retrieve it, even if it cost them a couple hundred thousand dollars.

The FBI, the perpetrator's attorney, and Smith worked out a method of exchange in the event an agreement could be reached. The perpetrator, through his attorney, would make the paintings available "somewhere in the Eastern (judicial) District of Michigan." The perpetrator would either tell the FBI exactly where they were or provide enough information for a search warrant that would result in their recovery. Simultaneously, a check would be made out to the perpetrator's attorney and placed in escrow with the FBI. Home Insurance would have forty-eight hours to authenticate the paintings. Once the insurer accepted the paintings, the check would be cashed and the money turned over to the perpetrator.

Queried whether such an arrangement was normal in respect to stolen objects of value, Smith replied, "There is no normal deal." Then he corrected himself. "You could say that they normally turn out to be disasters."

The Detroit deal didn't result in anyone getting ripped off or killed, but it didn't work either.

"My client and the FBI discussed whether any reward should be offered for the return of the paintings, and ultimately my client decided against it," says Smith. "A claim or maybe two claims had already been processed, and the insurer decided that would be the end of it as far as they were concerned."

According to Bonnie Lindberg, the insurer was willing to go through with the deal, but Brown & Bigelow balked. As she recalls, the executive who made that decision said the company had already bought the paintings once, so why should they buy them again.

There was one more attempt at a deal after that one fell through. Early in 1986, a private investigator the Lindbergs had hired contacted Bonnie and told her that organized crime figures in Detroit had the paintings.

"I got on the phone with a lawyer who said he represented the mob," says Bonnie. "The name 'Rockwell' was never spoken. He actually never uttered the word 'paintings.' It was 'the property,' or 'the goods,' all very pulp-novelish. I just said we'd have to think about it, and called the FBI. They told us not to do it, to leave it alone. I remember thinking that they might still be hoping to make a deal, and they didn't want us involved. What they actually said was that if we succeeded we would be in possession of stolen property, because the insurer owned the paintings. I assumed he was talking about Brown & Bigelow's paintings. I knew they'd been paid, but I didn't know that we'd been paid as well. I suppose I would have found out pretty quickly if there'd been any serious conversation about getting them back, but that never happened."

A letter addressed to the lawyer who represented the perpetrator (name redacted), dated April 9, 1986, concludes: "The Detroit office of the Federal Bureau of Investigation will make no further attempts to contact either Brown and Bigelow or Home Insurance regarding this matter.—Thank You for your assistance, Kenneth P. Walton, Special Agent in Charge, Michigan Division, Federal Bureau of Investigation."

In January 1987, the Minneapolis office issued a memo suggesting that the case be closed because "the Statute of Limitations has run, the stolen paintings have not been recovered and efforts to assist in arrangements to recover the paintings have been unsuccessful."

But if the investigators were unsuccessful, the thieves they were investigating hadn't exactly succeeded. Their efforts to collect a reward had come to nothing. One of them had tried to trade the paintings for a plea bargain and been rebuffed.

The evidence indicates that in 1986, the man who relocated to Detroit turned the paintings over to representatives of the Miami mob in return for a relatively small fee, which he split with his cohorts. They'd had eight years to hit the jackpot, but they failed. That ended the Minneapolis gang's involvement with the paintings.

The three who are still living are enjoying quiet retirements—one on the East Coast, two in the Twin Cities area.

13

BY THE LATE 1980S ELAYNE HAD BEGUN TURNING GALLERY affairs over to her daughter, but it was a drawn-out process. She never informed Bonnie that Home Insurance had paid a $34,500 claim for the stolen Date Paintings in 1978.

"I wasn't much involved when the payment came," Bonnie explains, "and by the time I was, it probably slipped her mind. You know, the robbery was a big dramatic event, but it wasn't front and center forever. We had a gallery to run, and frankly, we were doing quite well and it took most of our time and energy just to keep up. As I learned more about the business, I took on a greater role. My dad stepped in as well, so for a while there the three of us were equal partners."

According to Gary Lindberg, his parents quickly came to terms with the fact that the paintings had been stolen from their gallery.

"Their attitude was, they'd done everything they

could to make the place secure so they didn't need to beat themselves up over it. But they didn't exactly put it behind them either. They remained curious bordering on obsessed about what became of the paintings, where they were, who had them, and that never changed even though they were getting older."

It was an attitude the whole family shared, and the irony of it isn't lost on Bonnie. Frustration and a heartfelt wish for closure were part of it, but so was an unmistakable intoxication with the mystery and intrigue the situation generated. And kept on generating. After the initial rush of events, it took on a rhythm of its own.

"It would die out for a while, and all of a sudden something else would pop up, and it was like, 'Okay, let's see where this leads.' And of course we'd call the FBI every time. I guess we became a thorn in their side."

By 1990 Bonnie had major responsibility for the gallery's public relations, marketing and planning shows, and the increasingly difficult task of getting the FBI interested in tips that continued coming in.

"We'd tell them about things we heard, but it got so I couldn't even get an agent to return my phone call," she says. "It seemed like they'd closed the case and didn't want to reopen it. It was discouraging. I'd pretty much given up on it by 1991. Then we got a phone call from the Eleanor Ettinger Gallery in New York."

The Ettinger Gallery was the premier East Coast dealer in Norman Rockwell's work. According to the caller, Sotheby's in New York had been contacted by a person representing a recently widowed Argentinean woman who wanted to auction three Rockwell paintings. They had been part of her late husband's collection.

Sotheby's determined that the paintings had been stolen. They were "The Spirit of 1976," which had belonged to Brown & Bigelow, and the two Date Paintings that had belonged to the gallery.

"Barbara Ettinger told me that Sotheby's had put her in touch with the man in Argentina, and he wanted to do the right thing, so we should contact him. I can't remember the exact sequence of events, but at some point he called me. I believe Barbara Ettinger gave him my number."

The caller introduced himself as Mario Ravanaugh (another Latino/Irishman), a private investigator and collector of classic automobiles. He said he had some familiarity with the market in collectibles due to his avocation, but he pleaded ignorance about the value of the paintings and art in general. He said the widow who possessed the stolen painting did indeed want to do the right thing, and so did he, but there would be a "finder's fee" involved.

"The sum he mentioned was laughable, it was so exorbitant," says Bonnie.

She called the insurance company, which by then had been bought and sold twice, and was told that she would have to pay the reward. In its written response, the insurer said if she were to do so, and as a result recovered the paintings, the paintings would belong to their owners only after the insurer had been reimbursed for the settlement it had paid. The sum indicated was the amount paid to Brown & Bigelow, with no reference to any payment to the gallery.

Bonnie contacted the FBI. The Minneapolis office made note of the call, but there is no indication that they followed up.

"That ended that, as far as I was concerned," says Bonnie. "Whether there was actually a widow whose husband left her the paintings was never substantiated, but from then on we at least had an inkling that the paintings were in South America."

But how had they gotten there? By way of Portugal, if a fax from someone associated with the Schreiner Gallery in Lisbon, addressed to "Mrs Elayne," can be taken at face value. Dated April 16, 1993, it solicits Elayne

Lindberg's support in getting the paintings out of the hands of a "gang" in Brazil and bringing them "back to Portugal." In other faxes, the writer explains that this would be step one in a plan to return the paintings to their rightful owners.

Bonnie and her husband, Kevin Callahan, a frame-maker she met when he did work for the gallery, had taken over most of Elayne Galleries' affairs by the time the letter was received. Elayne died a year later.

14

MAJOR ART THEFTS ARE REDOLENT OF THE ERA IN WHICH they take place. The 1940s belong to the Nazis, who looted the great museums and homes of Europe with maniacal zeal, especially art belonging to Jews. More than twenty thousand stolen pieces were sent to Germany during World War II. Much of it was bound for the museums that Hitler dreamed about building once the thousand-year Reich was up and running, but the most coveted works landed in the private collections of Hitler, Goering, Rosenberg, and other party luminaries.

There is a famous photo of Goering in Paris's Galerie Jeu de Paume, looking over a painting he has just stolen. He has it propped on a chair, and in order to view it he is crouched in what must have been an uncomfortable position for a man of his girth. He looks pleased anyway. His aide can be seen in the background, pouring him a glass of champagne.

The list of paintings stolen by the Nazis and still missing includes works by Cezanne, Renoir, Bonnard, Sisley, and Manet. In his book *The Lost Museum,* Hector Feliciano reveals the complicity of Swiss and French financial institutions, collectors such as the Swiss arms manufacturer Emil Bührle, and many Parisian galleries in the thefts. "The war was a godsend for Paris's art market," writes Feliciano. "It brought an end to the crisis of the 1930s, when art prices declined by as much as seventy percent from what they'd been earlier; forcing a third of Paris's art galleries to close their doors."

In the 1970s, people wore mood rings and puzzled over Rubik's Cubes. Nixon shook hands with Mao, and Sadat shook hands with Begin. Smiley-face stickers competed with graffiti for public space. Airplanes were more like limousines than cattle cars. People dressed up for air travel. It had glamour and sex appeal. So did pilots and stewardesses.

The social conflicts and economic upheavals of the era were reflected in the art thefts as well as the art. The fake art scam that generated the Rockwell heist smacked of the oil jitters, a new form of anxiety that entered the culture with the OPEC embargo in 1973. Unlike disco balls and platform shoes, it came to stay.

The price of crude at the refinery level doubled in

1974. Gas lines, runaway inflation, and "stagflation" sent smart investors—and investors who just thought they were smart—hunting for a hedge.

Art galleries were one place they looked. Miami, the main entry point for cocaine, was another. Crude money-laundering schemes involving cocaine and art became commonplace as both commodities grew in value in counterpoint to an economy that was tanking. Cocaine, which cost about $1,500 per kilo to process in Colombia, sold for up to $50,000 per kilo in the United States. The problem was getting it into the country. Established distribution routes and sophisticated smuggling methods came later. It was a free-for-all in the 1970s, and major busts of airline employees occurred regularly at Miami International Airport. In 1977, Aero Cóndor Airlines of Peru almost lost its landing rights after two stewardesses were arrested in the act of smuggling cocaine. The method they employed is described in a court document relating to their unsuccessful appeal:

> After determining that nothing was concealed on the upper portion of Afanador's body, the female customs inspectors directed Afanador to lift her skirt and lower her girdle. After some confusion resulting from language difficulties, Afanador did so, revealing two packages, later determined to contain cocaine, one located on the body surface in the crotch area and one taped

slightly below the waist. Afanador then removed the packages and handed them to the customs inspector. A similar strip search of VidalGarcia, conducted somewhat later, revealed two packages carried in the same manner.

Airline employees were reputed to be eager customers of art galleries in the 1970s, too. "It didn't surprise me that a stewardess was involved in our situation," says Bonnie. "Art as an investment was really in vogue around that time, and people who'd never been interested in art were buying and selling. It could be anybody with some disposable income, but people in the airline industry were really into it. I remember that there was a gallery set up in O'Hare Airport in the seventies, and there were always four or five uniformed pilots and a few stewardesses looking at paintings. It was a kind of bazaar, and somehow you got the feeling that art was being purchased there for quick resale at the next layover. Of course the opportunity for fraud was obvious. Most of them couldn't tell an oil painting from a cheap print."

The Elayne Galleries theft was emblematic of its time and its place, but it wasn't the signature art theft of the 1970s. That honor belongs to a heist in Ireland engineered by a disaffected heiress acting on behalf of the Irish Republican Army.

Rose Dugdale was educated in private schools in England and France, earned an undergraduate degree in economics at Oxford, and by age thirty-three had become a militant feminist and devotee of many left-wing causes. Photos of her reveal a sharp-featured, dimple-cheeked young woman with sparkling eyes, a defiant grin, and a clenched fist raised above her flying locks. She's usually standing outside a courtroom.

Dugdale's career in crime began in 1973, when she and her boyfriend stole paintings and silver valued at more than $150,000 from her family's estate. They were soon arrested and brought to trial. Dugdale chose to defend herself, which gave her the opportunity to cross-examine her father. When the judge objected to her inquiries about the origins of the family's fortune, she replied: "This is a political trial. My father's life represents something alien to my own."

After the jury found her guilty, she thanked jurors for helping her transform herself "from a recalcitrant intellectual into a freedom fighter." That statement might have settled any doubts about her intentions. Nevertheless, she received a fine and a suspended sentence, while her boyfriend got four years. The judge explained that, in his opinion, Dugdale was an impressionable girl who had been led astray, and it was unlikely that she would commit another crime.

His Honour's deference must have infuriated her, but she buttoned her lip. She had taken up with an IRA man named Eddie Gallagher during the trial, and prison would have disrupted their plans.

In January 1974, three men and a woman posing as tourists booked a helicopter for a sightseeing trip over the Donegal area of Ireland. The pilot didn't ask why they brought four milk cans aboard, but he found out soon enough. They commandeered the aircraft shortly after takeoff, swooped down, and tried to hit a Royal Ulster Constabulary station with two of the cans, which were loaded with explosives. They missed, jettisoned the remaining cans when they began smoldering inside the helicopter, made a wobbly landing, and escaped. Based on the pilot's description, warrants were issued for the arrests of Dugdale and Gallagher.

The pair eluded the police, and not long after, Dugdale and three accomplices pulled off one of the century's biggest art thefts. The choice of victims was consistent with their dim view of the British ruling class in general, and Brits who buy Irish estates in particular.

Russborough House, where they struck, was the ancestral home of the Leesons, descendants of an officer in the army of William of Orange, a family that owed its fortune to the Protestant ascension. It is situated in the Wicklow Hills, a secluded region long cherished by

Irish poets and Irish gangsters for the same reason: it's easy to get lost there.

Lord Alfred Beit, heir to a South African diamond fortune, bought Russborough in 1952 to house the extensive art collection he and Lady Beit had accumulated. They purchased it on the basis of a photo, but once they laid eyes on their nineteen-room Palladian mansion, they decided to move in, along with their Rembrandts, their Goyas, their Vermeer, and a king's ransom in silver, bronze sculpture, and antique furniture. The value of art fluctuates considerably, but the collection was consistently estimated at more than $200 million. Nevertheless, they didn't give a thought to security, and for twenty-two years they didn't need to.

On the afternoon of April 26, 1974, Dugdale knocked on the service door of Russborough House and told the footman that her car had broken down. As she and the footman stood in the doorway, Dugdale's accomplices rushed in, waving pistols and demanding to be led to Lord and Lady Beit. They were guided to the library, where, amid shouts of "capitalist pig" (a ruse meant to suggest that Maoists were the culprits, not Irish nationalists), nobles and servants alike were bound hand and foot and gagged with stockings.

Dugdale showed her accomplices which paintings to snatch off the lavishly hung walls. The theft took ten minutes. They exited with nineteen works, including a Rembrandt sketch, Goya's portrait of Dona Antonia Zarate, and possibly the single most valuable painting in the world, Vermeer's "Lady Writing a Letter with Her Maid." News reports estimated the value of the stolen art at eight million pounds.

The paintings were meant to be held hostage for the freedom of IRA prisoners. It might have worked, but the moment the footman described the young woman who knocked at the service door, investigators knew who they were looking for. The thieves were captured and the paintings recovered a week later. At trial, Rose Dugdale pled "proudly and incorruptibly guilty" and was sentenced to nine years in prison.

That was the end of her career as an art thief (to date), but the well-publicized robbery she organized caught the eye of culprits with more conventional motivation. Russborough House was robbed three more times, most recently in 2002.

The thefts from Russborough House are chronicled in two books, *The Irish Game* by Matthew Hart and *The Rescue Artist* by Edward Dolnick. Both authors had access to Charley Hill, the Scotland Yard detective whose undercover work finding stolen art has made him internationally famous. Both books are excellent reads if you like true crime, and *The Irish Game* is even better if you're interested in a true criminal. Hart goes into some detail about Martin Cahill, the Dublin gangster who engineered the second theft. Cahill, aka The General—a nickname derived from his ability to assemble a gang for major heists—has been the subject of several biographies, a film, and a memoir by his daughter.

Cahill was a genuine eccentric. His connubial arrangement included his sister-in-law. His income from crime was said to be six figures per month, but he habitually broke into ordinary middle-class homes, alone, in the dead of night, and pilfered small objects for the thrill of it. His experiences growing up in a Dublin slum led him to conclude that there was no percentage in talking to a cop, a jailer, or anyone else in authority, ever, and as a teenager he reputedly ignored every word the warders uttered throughout an entire two-year stretch in an Irish reformatory. The police brought him in for interviews frequently as his career as the leading figure in Irish crime was getting under way, but they finally had to admit that his capacity for remaining silent exceeded theirs for making him talk, and they quit trying.

Thumbing his nose at authority was Cahill's primary motivation. It also seems clear that, in his mind at least, he was in an ongoing rivalry with the IRA to see who could defy the law more audaciously. He had been hearing of the 1974 robbery of Russborough House since he was a juvenile delinquent, and he knew that a second theft was right up his alley. The fact that the Beits had decided to make a gift of some of their most valuable works to the Irish National Gallery played into his hands as well, although it only became known in the aftermath of the crime. In the event, he not only robbed an iconic Irish estate of items of huge value, he robbed Ireland itself.

By the time he decided to make his move, in 1986, security at Russborough House was marginally better than it had been in 1974, but as if to counter such precautions, the Beits had decided to open their mansion to the public from Easter to November. In April, Cahill paid the one-pound admission and took the guided tour, taking note of where certain pieces were hung and which exits were handy. It is believed that he figured out how to foil the alarm system during this visit.

On the night of May 17, he and his gang broke into Russborough House and stole eighteen paintings. Their haul included the Vermeer that Dugdale and her IRA cohorts had stolen and a Goya, both of which were destined for the National Gallery.

Cahill had made off with fewer paintings than Dugdale, but their net worth exceeded the earlier robbery's because the art market had improved and so had the provenance of one of the key paintings. The

Vermeer had been stolen and recovered, which has the perverse effect of raising the value of a work of art. Couple that with the fact that the day after the robbery, Lord Beit told the press about the impending gift to the National Gallery, and Cahill could boast that he had bested the IRA.

He hid the paintings in the Wicklow Hills and began flaunting his success in a manner calculated to enrage the Irish police. They knew he was the culprit, and he knew they knew. What Cahill didn't know was that a flying squad of art recovery specialists from Scotland Yard would be leading the investigation, and they would bring their own cadre of snitches and undercover operatives with them.

Cahill's competition with the IRA blinded him to something that Hart calls "the snag that lies beneath the smooth surface of art crime." Art may be easy to steal, but it is hard to sell. That is especially true of the quality of art Cahill stole. The ownership of a globally acknowledged masterpiece is carefully documented. No one with an interest in art can acquire it and claim ignorance. That doesn't mean it can't be monetized, but doing so is far more difficult than selling a lesser-known work to an unwitting buyer at face value.

For the purposes of the stolen-art commerce, the news stories a major robbery generates serve as an appraisal. Headlines in the UK said the loot from Russborough House was worth in excess of $100 million. Seven percent of estimated value is about what thieves can expect from the black market when masterpieces are on offer. All they have to do is find a buyer. Such a person didn't exist in the Dublin underworld, so Cahill began putting out feelers through his connections on the mainland. Thus began a cat-and-mouse game that would take place on turf unfamiliar to him. He ultimately failed to monetize the art, but the methods he employed as he tried shed some light on the difficulties encountered by whoever came into possession of the Rockwell paintings.

The Rockwells presented a unique problem. They were as recognizable as any masterpiece, but the artist's work never had the same value in Europe that it has in the United States. After an initial spike following Rockwell's death, the prices his paintings commanded in the United States drifted downward. They surged again with the outpouring of patriotic sentiment that occurred after the attack on the World Trade Center and have continued to increase since, but between 1986, when the paintings left Detroit, and 1991, when they appeared in South America, his most sought-after work was selling in the mid-five figures.

15

ACCORDING TO THE SEVEN-PERCENT BLACK MARKET FOR-
mula, the eighteen paintings Cahill stole could have
netted him about $7 million. In fact, he managed to
sell only one, and whatever it netted (the investigators
never found out), it cost him far more. In 1987, Cahill
tried to do business with a Dutch con man who had
been turned by the Irish police. In September of that
year he escaped the trap they set for him, and made
the police look silly in the process, but he still hadn't
monetized the loot.

An arrangement he tried to reach with a crooked
London art dealer resulted in the recovery of four of
the paintings by Scotland Yard. He comforted himself
with the knowledge that he had fourteen more, including the Vermeer. Over the next few years he tried to
unload them several times, including one failed deal
with the IRA. When that fell through he turned to a
Protestant paramilitary group in Northern Ireland,

the Ulster Volunteer Force. In 1989, he sold one of the paintings, Gabriel Metsu's "A Woman Reading a Letter," to the UVF.

A few months later, Turkish authorities arrested a UVF man and two Turkish art dealers in an Istanbul hotel room, where they had been tipped that a sale was taking place. The Metsu painting was recovered. Publicity around that bust put a dent in Cahill's reputation. It seemed that the man whom many Dubliners lionized for his code and his courage was willing to do anything for a buck, even if it meant furthering the aims of a Protestant militia.

By 1993, the task of turning the paintings into something of value had Cahill's full attention. A deal he tried to put together woke investigators up to the fact that the stolen-art market had changed.

Before their undercover agent told them what Cahill was doing, police believed that stolen art could be monetized in only three ways: (1) through prearranged sale to a fence, who would engineer its entry into the legitimate market by initiating a series of documented sales, thereby creating a provenance—a method that worked best when the art was desirable but not well known; (2) by stealing art on contract for a wealthy collector; and (3) by selling it to criminals for cash that needed laundering, the recipient's goal being to resell it for clean cash. The Scotland Yard squad became aware of a variation on that method. They discovered that some criminals, most notably Colombian drug dealers, were collecting art for status. In their world, stolen art had more cachet than art that was legitimately acquired.

In 1993, Cahill introduced investigators to a fourth method, which solved the problem posed by masterpieces. Working through a crooked Belgian diamond dealer, he made a deal in which four of the Beit paintings, including the Vermeer, would be accepted as collateral on a drug transaction. In return for the paintings, he would receive one million dollars' worth of heroin. It would be his choice whether to retrieve the art for that sum or leave the paintings as payment in full. Apparently the suppliers were confident in their ability to ransom the art, which raises the question, who has that kind of money and might be willing to part with it for such a purpose? The Italian Mafia is said to have identified one such entity.

The Vatican has all but confirmed rumors that it has been in off-and-on negotiations with mafiosi for decades, with the goal of recovering Caravaggio's "Nativity with St. Francis and St. Lawrence," stolen from a church in Palermo in 1969. Governments, multinational corporations, and foundations are all considered approachable when a national treasure, or a painting

such as the Vermeer (one of thirty-four the artist painted in his lifetime), are at stake.

Great art is timeless, and negotiations over its recovery, such as those between the Roman Catholic
Church and the Mafia, can take on that same quality. One thing that prolongs them is the fact that the
only real threat the possessors of the art can wield, that
they'll destroy it, is an empty one, so neither side is in
any rush to make a deal. The negotiations take place
between institutions that will outlive the individuals
involved in the bargaining.

16

THE BELGIAN DIAMOND DEALER'S ORGANIZATION HAD been infiltrated by Scotland Yard, so the details of the agreement he and Cahill struck were known to investigators. They even drew up an elaborate chart showing the flow of stolen art and money to and from various locales—Dublin, Antigua, the Isle of Man, Istanbul—that would result if the deal went as planned. But it didn't. In August 1993, the paintings were recovered in the trunk of a car at the Antwerp airport, the culmination of an undercover operation. Several arrests were made. Cahill was in Ireland when the bust occurred, and the police were unable to connect him to the paintings, so he got to thumb his nose at them one last time. He was assassinated in 1994. The Provisional IRA took credit, citing his involvement with the Ulster Volunteer Force, which began when he sold that organization the Metsu.

Cahill's reputation as a legendary Irish criminal had been established long before he robbed Russborough House, but investigators are likely to remember him as the man who made stolen art a commodity of exchange on the illicit market. It changed the paradigm, and may have led directly to the theft of many masterpieces, including the Van Goghs stolen from the Van Gogh Museum in Amsterdam in 2002 and the paintings by Dali, Picasso, Matisse, and Monet taken from the Chácara do Céu Museum in Rio de Janeiro in 2006. Investigators assume that the art stolen from the Gardner Museum in Boston in 1990 was ultimately used to purchase drugs or firearms.

Pity the poor thief who was trying to use Rockwell paintings stolen from Elayne Galleries as collateral for a major drug purchase in the 1980s. They were immediately recognizable to anyone who was knowledgeable about art, but their value was not on par with a masterpiece. That was especially true in Europe.

In 1975, one of Rockwell's most famous paintings, an oil original for a 1963 *Saturday Evening Post* cover that depicted an African American girl being escorted by U.S. marshals to her first day at an all-white school, sold for $35,000. The Rockwells stolen from Elayne Galleries were worth less than that because they didn't have the same historical significance. According to the seven-percent black market formula, they were collectively worth about $15,000 in the United States, maybe half that in Europe.

Twenty years later it would have been a different story. The recollections of the aforementioned Robert Rosenblum exemplify the critical reappraisal of Rockwell's status that led to a steady increase in the value of his paintings.

"I had been taught to look down my nose at Rockwell, but then, I had to ask myself why," Rosenblum wrote in 1998. "If it had already become respectable to scrutinize and admire the infinite detail, dramatic staging, narrative intrigues, and disguised symbols of Victorian-genre paintings, why couldn't the same standards apply here? I for one am happy now to love Rockwell for his own sake. We have a newborn Rockwell who can no longer be looked at with sneering condescension and might well become an indispensable part of art history."

The details Rosenblum references—he calls them "a mind-boggling abundance of tiny observations"—were key elements in Rockwell's art. He used them to tell stories in his paintings, and those stories, his admirers and detractors agree, are quintessentially American. A foreigner might recognize them as part of a nostalgic re-creation of a time and a place, but the images would hardly evoke the emotional response that they have for Americans.

"Norman told me how he used details when he worked," says Ron Ringling, a Minneapolis-area Rockwell collector. "He said, 'When I see something I like, I paint it on canvas. When you see something you like, you paint it in your memory, but the best way to do either thing is to remember some details. That's how I start on these paintings. I have a couple of details that I've committed to memory, and I take it from there.'"

Ringling looks back on that conversation with Rockwell as one of the best experiences of his life. The artist was in a wheelchair with a blanket over his lap when it took place, and obviously not well. He died a few months later. The fact that Ringling was at the artist's home in Stockbridge, Massachusetts, when they spoke is indicative of something else that made the stolen Rockwells more valuable in the United States than they were in Europe. People who collect his work are a little bit clubby. They tend to feel a personal involvement with the world Rockwell created in his art.

Ringling has made several pilgrimages to Arlington, Vermont, and across the Battenkill River to Stockbridge, where Rockwell spent his final years. In the summer of

1978, Ringling was driving down a country road near Arlington when he saw a sign: Rockwell Memorabilia Museum.

"It was just an old house, no security really, and there were about twenty of Norm's pieces on display there. Some were painted and some were pencil drawings. I asked the lady who was running the place where she got them."

She explained that they were studies for *Saturday Evening Post* covers. They belonged to the local people who appeared in them and ultimately appeared in the painting Rockwell used them to execute. The artist often made gifts of the sketches to his models, who treasured them mostly for the near-photographic likeness of their visage. When Ringling came across those pieces, they were considered mere curiosities with personal meaning for the owners but of little value otherwise. Ringling told the proprietor of the museum that if the owners wanted to sell them, he might be interested in buying.

Later that year, he purchased five of the pieces for $40,000. He's since sold them all, several through Elayne Galleries. In the last decade or so, their value has increased considerably because they function as illustrations of how the artist worked.

"I'd say they're worth three times what I sold them for at minimum," he says.

Two of the pieces he sold depict scenes from a carnival that the original owner's family operated around New England for years. In the corner of one of those sketches there appears the unmistakable likeness of someone whose name is familiar to all Rockwell aficionados: Gene Pelham.

Pelham was a fellow cover artist for the *Post* who eventually became Rockwell's photographer and assistant. The two were friends for years, then their friendship ended, apparently because Pelham believed he should have gotten more recognition for his assistance. His face appears in many Rockwell paintings.

Ringling met Pelham when he went to Arlington to pick up the sketches he'd purchased from the Memorabilia Museum. "I was told he might have some Rockwells he'd be willing to sell," says Ringling. "The librarian at the town library said to look him up. In fact, he introduced me to Gene's wife right there in the library, and she told me Gene was down in their car waiting for her. So I went out and talked to him."

Pelham was standoffish at first but eventually invited Ringling to his house for a drink. They had several drinks and a long, rambling conversation during which Pelham revealed more than a little animosity toward his old friend.

"There were clearly some hard feelings on Gene's

part," says Ringling. "He said, 'Norm, he just pulled out and left me, went to Stockbridge and I never heard from him again.' I suppose Norm went over there to retire and just lost contact, but Gene took it personally. He told me he didn't really have any of Norman's paintings to sell. 'I have a few sketches,' he said, 'but my kids want those.'"

Ringling spent the night in Pelham's spare bedroom. The next morning over breakfast Pelham admitted that he hadn't been totally honest about possessing Rockwell paintings.

"We finished eating, went outside, and he reached into a crawl space under his house and pulled out a tube," says Ringling. "I don't know if it was cardboard or what, but he had two paintings in there, and then he said he had three more stored down at the bank. He never did tell me why some of them were in storage, and some were just shoved under the house. But they were all in good condition. I bought all five of them for $60,000."

Ringling has bought and sold many Rockwell paintings over the years. He chuckles when he thinks about what some of them are worth now, but it's clear that he isn't in it for the money. Queried about why he is so fond of Rockwell's work, he replies, "Norman painted the way we remember it. Not necessarily the way it was, but the way we like to remember it. The experience of looking at one of his paintings is—well, it's incredible. Just incredible."

But Ringling does wince a bit when he thinks about one painting that got away. He bought it in 1980, from a dealer in Chicago who was representing the widow of a former president of Montgomery Ward & Company. It depicted an elderly woman sitting in an attic. "She has a trunk open and she's reading a letter she's taken out of it," says Ringling. "There's kind of a distant look on her face, like she's reliving the past. It was done as a cover for a Ward's catalogue, in the 1940s I believe, but it had been hanging in their living room all that time, and it was in absolutely mint condition."

Ringling bought it for $50,000 and sold it a few years later for $80,000.

"You couldn't buy it for a million dollars today," he says.

In 2006, Sotheby's sold a Rockwell titled "Breaking Home Ties" for more than $15 million.

17

THE EVIDENCE SUGGESTS THAT THE STOLEN PAINTINGS, minus the "Renoir," which has never surfaced again, made their way to Lisbon. After failing to unload them there, the organized crime figures who controlled them must have concluded that if they were to realize anything at all on their sale, the paintings had to re-enter the New World.

Whether or not they were actually in Argentina in 1991, when the car collector who wanted to do the right thing contacted Sotheby's, is an open question. They had certainly entered Brazil by 1993. Three faxes were sent to Elayne Galleries in the spring of that year, all by a man who represented himself as interested in making sure the paintings were returned to their rightful owners. The faxes were on the letterhead of Galerie Schreiner, Inc., a company with galleries in Lisbon, Basel, and New York. The sender was in Lisbon. He wanted to arrange the return of the paintings to Portugal, where he would set up a sting operation that would result in their recovery.

"Dear Mrs Elayne," says the first fax, dated April 28, 1993, "The case is too complicated to deal with alone. We'll have to join forces. I fear we have to deal with a gang!"

"The day after we got that fax, I got a phone call from the gallery owner himself," says Bonnie. "He wanted to make certain we were the people who owned the Rockwells. I told him we were, and he said, 'I believe your paintings are being held by the federal police in Brazil.' So first it's a gang, then it's the federal police. Of course, later on we came to understand that in Brazil it's a thin line."

The caller claimed that he was personally acquainted with the president of Portugal and had contacts in Brazil who would be able to obtain the paintings from the police. He was worried that his involvement in the situation might damage his reputation, but he was willing to risk it if the paintings could be recovered.

"That same day I got a call from a fellow named Fulvio Minetti," says Bonnie. "He was a State Farm Insurance agent in Las Vegas, but he owned a travel agency and a money exchange in Rio de Janeiro as well. He told me pretty much the same story as the gallery owner, that the Rockwell paintings were in the hands of the Brazilian federal police. So I had information from two independent sources who said the same thing: The paintings are in Rio, and the police have them."

Minetti claimed to have some shady Brazilian contacts who could get their hands on the paintings and said he would call again soon. At that point no deal had been discussed, but Minetti clearly had one in mind.

Bonnie notified the FBI's Minneapolis office. "They were simply not interested," she says. "It made me mad. I'd heard that they'd organized an FBI art crime team in Washington, and somehow I found out how to reach them and managed to get someone on the phone. I explained what was going on, and within hours a local agent came to the gallery. He told me to get as much information as I could from the people I was in touch with, but he said he was skeptical that any of it was real."

She made further inquiries of the Home Insurance Company, based on her hunch that this time something might come of the contacts. She said she needed the files because her mother had passed away, and they were now her only reference if questions about ownership of any of the paintings were to arise. They sent a copy of the $90,000 claim paid to Brown & Bigelow and said that was the extent of it, according to their records.

Bonnie contacted Minetti and told him exactly what was going on. Minetti was upset that the FBI was in-

Photo sent from Brazil in 1993, with a newspaper in the background to demonstrate that the painting was there at that time and place

volved. In order not to be seen as a double-crosser, he would have to tell his Brazilian contacts about their involvement, he said, and they might back out. Nevertheless, he was open to offering some proof that the paintings were in Rio, and in reasonable condition.

"I guess it was my idea to have photos taken of them along with a newspaper with that day's date showing," says Bonnie. "I figured, why not? They were 'hostages,' after all."

To her surprise, and the FBI's, the photos soon arrived in the mail. The dated newspaper was clearly visible in each photo, and there was enough detail to identify the paintings as the ones that were stolen in 1978.

"You could see some worn areas around the stretcher marks that I remembered," Bonnie explains. "They were unquestionably the real thing. It was pretty exciting."

The FBI agent told her to find out what Minetti and his contacts wanted, but he also explained a fundamental problem relating to the paintings' whereabouts.

According to a UNESCO agreement that law enforcement agencies rely upon in international cases, UNESCO member states require the recipients of stolen art to give it up, even if it was acquired in good faith. But Brazil was not a member state of UNESCO, which meant that there were no legal means by which the U.S. government could help get the paintings back.

On May 17 a fax arrived from Galerie Schreiner, in which the writer claimed that his "correspondent in Brazil" had concluded that it would be dangerous to reveal the names of the people who were involved on his end. The FBI suggested ignoring him. On June 5 he said he needed to hear from Mrs. Elayne "regarding different aspects of the problem Rockwell." He couldn't keep matters on hold much longer without raising suspicions, and if he didn't receive instructions pretty soon he would have "no other choice but to retreat from the whole matter."

That was the last they heard from Galerie Schreiner.

Minetti and Bonnie stayed in touch. After three months of frequent phone calls, he finally explained what he had in mind. He proposed that Bonnie come to Rio with half a million dollars in cash, out of which he would take a ten-percent finder's fee. The paintings would be returned as soon as the money was paid.

"Well, that wasn't going to happen," Bonnie says, "but the FBI wanted me to string him along, so I didn't act too shocked."

There were a few more calls, in which some haggling took place. By July 5, 1993, the price was down to $250,000, but Minetti warned that matters had to be brought to a swift conclusion. One of the paintings had been pledged against a loan that came due on July 15, and the lender was eager to get his hands on it.

There was discussion of the FBI sending a female agent posing as Bonnie to Brazil, but it was nixed before it got off the ground. The agency said they would make some efforts through Interpol. Nothing came of that either.

"Obviously I couldn't come up with the kind of money he was talking about, the insurer wouldn't help, and the FBI couldn't make anything happen, so things just sort of wound down," Bonnie says. "Eventually, maybe three or four months later, an FBI man came to the gallery. He handed me a folder of documents concerning the whole sequence of events starting from the first fax, and said there was nothing more they could do. 'You mean I'm on my own?' I asked him, and he said, 'Yes, you're on your own.'"

Bonnie describes her state of mind at that point as "worn out." She had her hopes up many times, and nothing had come of it. Furthermore, she had no idea who she had been dealing with, but they knew who she was and how to find her, and they didn't seem like nice people. It echoed something she felt fifteen years before, immediately after the theft.

"The TV stations were all there, and you know, you're upset and not thinking clearly, and I told one of them we had the license number of the thieves' car. Well, they led with that information along with a picture of me, and kept leading with it for days. We couldn't get them to take it off the air. So I'm thinking, whoever did this knows that I know, they know where to find me, and this is a big crime. These are real criminals. I was scared. Then fifteen years pass and all of a sudden it's South American gangsters who have my address. I said to myself, 'This is it. I'm done.'"

In 1995, Maureen Hennessey, curator of the Norman Rockwell Museum in Stockbridge, Massachusetts, called the gallery. He said he had received a letter from a man in Brazil who claimed to have the paintings and was willing to sell them. Bonnie thanked him for the information but didn't follow up. A few months later a fax came from a lawyer in Florida who claimed to represent someone who had information about the stolen Rockwells.

"I can't even remember his name," she says. "I was determined to ignore him. He made other attempts, but I didn't keep track because I honestly wanted it to be over."

Then one day she picked up the phone at the gallery, and the person on the other end said, "I have a friend who's been trying to contact you and you won't respond." Before she could hang up he explained that he was a South American residing in Washington, DC, a reputable, hard-working person.

"He said he installed draperies at embassies all over the world, if you can imagine that," says Bonnie. "But there was something about the guy, his voice or whatever, that made me think he was sincere. So, it was here we go again."

The drapery hanger said he had a college friend, Brazilian by birth but presently living in Florida, who wanted badly to speak to her. His name was Luis Palma. That was how the end game began.

18

PALMA APPEARED TO BE AN HONEST BROKER. HE SAID he represented the man who purchased five of the Rockwells from a Brazilian immigration official, among them the two that belonged to the gallery. He admitted that he expected to collect some money if a deal could be arranged, but it would come from the seller. There was no specific price mentioned, but Palma indicated that it would not be as outlandish as previous offers.

Subsequent conversations revealed how the paintings got to Brazil. They had entered in possession of a man who arrived at the Sao Paulo airport on an international flight. Customs officials discovered the paintings when they screened a large package he was carrying. The paintings were confiscated and ended up in possession of the federal police, but the man was not detained.

Why would customs seize the paintings as if they were contraband, then send the person who possessed them on his way? According to the FBI files, "The paintings paid for his entry into Brazil."

Brazil's constitution forbids extradition of its citizens to other countries, and fugitives often seek citizenship for that reason. Becoming a citizen of Brazil can be difficult and time-consuming, but payments to certain agencies can expedite the process, among them the federal police and the Department of Immigration and Visa Services.

According to Palma, the customs agent at the airport turned the paintings over to an immigration official whose husband was a federal policeman. He initially tried to sell the paintings through his underworld connections but eventually contacted a wealthy man, a legitimate art collector, who purchased five of them. The other two appear to have been used by someone as collateral for a loan.

The art collector had enlisted the aid of his friend Luis Palma in finding out if the paintings were stolen. When Palma discovered they were, the collector asked him to act as middleman in an attempt to get them back to their rightful owners.

The first thing Bonnie asked Palma was what proof he could offer that the collector was real and that the paintings were in his possession.

What proof do you want? he asked.

"I suggested that he send us one of the paintings," says Gary Lindberg, "but he told us that wasn't likely to happen, so we asked for photos."

Soon several crisp, detailed photos arrived, taken against the backdrop of what appeared to be some kind of redoubt in the rain forest. The telltale stretcher marks were present, and the paintings appeared to be in good condition. The collector himself, a portly man who appeared to be about fifty, was holding a painting in one of the photos.

"We didn't know his name at that point," Bonnie says. "I was thinking he's either awfully stupid for sending us a picture of himself, or he feels well protected down there. But we were satisfied that Palma had been truthful. I contacted the insurer again, and they told me again that there was no reward money, which was no surprise, but I wanted to make sure they were in the loop. I had a feeling that this time it might come to something, and I didn't want any trouble with them."

There were more phone calls. Eventually Palma revealed the name of the man he represented, Jose Carneiro, an art historian and teacher as well as a collector, who owned a private school in a town outside of Rio. Palma removed himself from the situation, and the Lindbergs began talking to Carneiro directly.

"I could tell we were dealing with a different kind

of person than I'd gotten used to," says Bonnie. "Was he a good guy? Well, if he was a really good guy he would have just sent the paintings back. Let's just say he wasn't a bad guy."

It was a slow process, and Bonnie soon asked her brother to take over what would prove to be a prolonged negotiation.

"It was kind of nerve-racking," says Gary, "but I found it fascinating. It was the culmination of twenty years chasing a ghost."

Information came one tidbit at a time. Sometimes months would go by without contact, but gradually Gary was able to put together a picture of the man he was dealing with. Carneiro, he came to believe, was conflicted about a situation that he hadn't fully understood until after he got into it. He was painfully aware that regardless of the legalities, he was not occupying the moral high ground. He had no intention of giving the paintings away, but he didn't seem to be in it for the last possible dollar either.

"It looked to me like his reputation was more important to him than any money he would get," Gary says. "He as much as admitted that, and he knew he had limited options as to what he could do with the paintings."

Carneiro let it be known that he was in New York

occasionally for art auctions and eventually agreed to meet there to discuss things in person. In May 1998, the three of them rendezvoused in a hotel coffee shop in Manhattan.

The Lindbergs had sent photos of themselves to Carneiro so he would recognize them, but there was no mistaking him. They spotted him from the door, a husky, Latin fellow wearing an expensive-looking suit and tapping his ring-bejeweled fingers on the table nervously as he waited. He rose when they approached and introduced himself. His English was accented, but quite understandable. He was about five feet six inches, and he bore a passing resemblance to the Mexican artist Diego Rivera.

"He was elegant, in a way," Bonnie recalls, "well dressed, polite. I suppose he was trying to make a good impression, and I'd have to say that he did."

"He came across as a business executive, very much so," says Gary. "He took great pains to present himself that way—the whole power executive thing. And he emphasized how very important it was to him that we believe he had no knowledge that the paintings were stolen when he bought them."

Carneiro professed great admiration for all things American, especially Norman Rockwell. He said he appreciated Rockwell in a way few people foreign to the United States did. He had paid a great deal for the paintings because he cherished the artist and everything embodied in his work.

"It was almost comical," says Gary, "and to this day I can't make up my mind if he was sincere or not."

Carneiro told them he traded a Rolls-Royce automobile and other items of value, along with some cash, for the paintings. He declined to estimate the total value of the exchange. He indicated that he knew the situation was favorable for him because Brazil was not party to the UNESCO agreement and he had acquired the paintings legally according to the applicable laws.

"Nevertheless," he said, "I was duped, and it embarrasses me to say so. I'm an art dealer, I should have known better, but my great admiration for the artist blinded me to the nature of this affair."

He explained that not long after he acquired the paintings, he began to have suspicions. He sent a letter to the Art Loss Register and received written assurance that the paintings weren't listed. Nevertheless, he contacted his friend Luis Palma in Florida and asked him to make inquiries of the Rockwell Museum. The curator told Palma that the paintings had indeed been stolen and provided contact information for Elayne Galleries.

"What he told us was plausible," according to Bonnie. "The register was started shortly after the theft.

I just assumed that the FBI or the insurer would get them listed, and I suppose they thought we would, so it fell through the cracks. If you took him at his word, you could say he had gone the extra mile to find out the truth."

"I still have some suspicions myself," says Gary. "This guy was very smart, there is no question about that. He might have been told that the art was stolen by the person he bought it from, and even if he wasn't told he had suspicions."

The discussion in New York went on for hours. Carneiro continued to stress the importance of his image. In the course of the conversation, he disclosed that his wealth and status were less dependent on his art collection and his art dealing than they were on the private school he owned and operated. He said the wealthy Brazilians who sent their children to be educated by him would be put off if he became involved in any scandal.

"So what can we do?" Gary asked. "Something has to be done, because the paintings are ours."

"No," Carneiro replied. "The paintings are mine. I have a bill of sale, and the law in Brazil is entirely on my side. I will, however, sell them back to you."

They began to discuss a deal. Gary made it clear that they wouldn't go ahead with any arrangement without proof positive that the paintings were real. "I told him the photos looked authentic, but when all was said and done they were just photos and we wanted to see a painting. Otherwise we'd be buying a pig in a poke."

Carneiro was displeased. He wondered if such a thing could be accomplished or if it was too much of an impediment. Gary suggested that it would work if Carneiro relied on their word, which he should do, since all of them were honorable people. He could ship a painting to the gallery for authentication. The Lindbergs would agree to send it back.

"He kind of smiled and said, 'No,'" says Gary, "but we began to talk about some variations on that idea."

They agreed that shipping a painting to the United States only to send it back again didn't make sense, but Carneiro said he was open to sending one painting to stay as part of a deal for both.

They soon struck a bargain. One of the Date Paintings would be shipped to the gallery for inspection. If it proved authentic, $40,000 would be wired to a bank account in Miami and forwarded to Carneiro.

They agreed on the same price for the second painting, but Carneiro balked at going through the same process in order to get his money. He said that sending the first painting before he saw any cash would be a gesture of good faith, and the Lindbergs should make a gesture of their own in regard to the second painting.

"I suggested that maybe we should come down to his place, at our own expense, and look at it there," says Gary. "That way we could authenticate all the paintings he had, which might help him sell the rest too. I could see the wheels turning for a few moments, and he said, 'Yes, that will work.'"

They agreed that Carneiro would set the time for the trip and figure out where they would meet and how they would get to where the paintings were kept without breaching any security. Carneiro wanted the whereabouts of the paintings kept secret because of their value and because he feared that despite the law, diplomatic pressure could lead the Brazilian authorities to try to seize them.

"I had visions of being led into the jungle blindfolded," Gary says, "but he wasn't quite that secretive. He explained that he had a home in Teresopolis, about sixty miles outside Rio, and that's where we'd be going. He told us we'd hear from him soon, and we parted on good terms."

"My heart was pounding like crazy," says Bonnie. "Twenty years had passed, and we were on the brink of succeeding. My mom hadn't lived to see it, but it looked like my dad would. It was a really good feeling."

Elayne Lindberg would have been proud of the idea her daughter had shortly after she returned to Minneapolis. She contacted a local TV station, KARE 11, and asked if they were interested in filming the return of the first painting and maybe even tagging along on the trip to Brazil. They agreed, and planned a two-part series that would air during sweeps week in February 1999.

Bonnie told the FBI in Minneapolis what was in the works. They didn't offer any help, but they didn't interfere either.

It wasn't long before an invitation to come to Rio arrived. They set a date. Carneiro initially balked at television coverage, but Gary convinced him it was a smart move, considering his concerns.

"I told him that it would be an opportunity to make sure his reputation didn't suffer. Instead of being portrayed simply as someone who'd sold stolen art back to its rightful owners, he'd be able to explain himself right there, on his own home ground, where nothing could go wrong. It took some back and forth but eventually he said, 'Why not? Bring yourselves, bring the TV crew and their cameras. Let's do it.'"

19

SHORTLY BEFORE CHRISTMAS 1998, AROUND THE TIME that Bonnie and Gary Lindberg were finalizing plans to go to Rio, a man came into an art gallery in Philadelphia with two Norman Rockwell paintings. He wanted them authenticated, appraised, and possibly sold.

"I can't remember his name or what he looked like—it's been such a long time," says the gallery's owner, George Turak. "But I do remember what he told me."

The man said he was originally from Philadelphia and had come to town from Brazil for the holidays to visit his brother, a city policeman. He claimed he worked for a bank in Brazil and explained that the Rockwell paintings had been pledged as collateral against a loan by someone who died while the loan was outstanding. He had brought the paintings with him in hopes of recouping some of the bank's money.

The two paintings were Bob Horvath's "She's My Baby," and "Lickin' Good Bath," which had belonged to

Brown & Bigelow. They had been rolled up in a brief-case, but they appeared to be in good condition.

Turak consulted a two-volume catalogue raisonné of Rockwell's work published by the Rockwell Museum and discovered that those two paintings, along with five more, were stolen from Elayne Galleries in 1978. "I called Bob Wittman over at the FBI right away," says Turak.

A few years before, Turak had helped special agent Robert Wittman when he was working on a theft from a Philadelphia museum, and the two had struck up a friendship. Wittman went on to found the FBI's art crime team. He was aware of the Minneapolis case, although he hadn't worked it.

Wittman arranged to have the two Rockwell paintings confiscated. It fell to Turak to inform the banker from Brazil.

"I called him right after Christmas and gave him the bad news. I said, 'You've got a couple stolen paintings here, and I have to turn them over to the authorities. Sorry, but I don't mess with this stuff.' He said, 'Do the right thing,' which to me meant 'Hand them over to the Feds,' but I got the feeling that to him it meant, 'Give them back to me.'"

Turak never heard from him again after the paintings were seized. The Philadelphia office of the FBI issued a press release announcing their recovery. It noted that the unnamed individual who brought them to Turak's gallery cooperated fully with the return of the art work and would not be charged with a crime.

The release goes into some detail about the paintings. "'She's My Baby' graced the cover of the June 4, 1927, issue of the *Saturday Evening Post*," it says. "'Lickin' Good Bath' was used in a calendar designed by Brown & Bigelow for the winter scene (January-February-March) 1954."

The paintings were displayed in a conference room at the FBI's offices. The public was invited and encouraged to take photos.

In September 1999, the Minneapolis office of the FBI returned the paintings to their owners. Phil Jungwirth, senior vice president of Brown & Bigelow, expressed his gratitude publicly, saying, "This is a treasure. Norman Rockwell is a piece of Americana that can't be duplicated."

The owner of "She's My Baby" sent Minneapolis attorney Dennis Peterson to pick up his painting. Peterson told the *St. Paul Pioneer Press* that his client preferred not to be identified. Contacted recently, Peterson says he is still not at liberty to disclose the owner's name. Bob Horvath owned the painting when it was stolen.

Shortly after the paintings were seized in Philadelphia, Wittman read the bureau's files on the Elayne Galleries theft (sans redactions, of course, but he steadfastly and good-naturedly refused to fill in any blanks throughout three interviews). He decided to ask a federal prosecutor about reopening the investigation. Assistant U.S. Attorney David Hall was assigned to work with Wittman. They soon found out that the remaining paintings were in the possession of a Brazilian art collector named Jose Carneiro.

They contacted law enforcement authorities in Brazil and began making plans that would require their cooperation. Discussions were then under way about a mutual legal assistance treaty between the United States and Brazil. Wittman assumed that those talks would work in their favor. The treaty, which gives the FBI leverage in situations like the one posed by Carneiro's possession of the stolen Rockwells, wasn't finalized until 2001.

The Minneapolis office of the FBI got Wittman and Hall up to speed on the Lindbergs' plans, which Wittman found alarming, especially the part about the TV station. He feared the publicity that a U.S. TV crew would stir up in Brazil would spoil his investigation, and maybe even torpedo the treaty negotiations.

"Bonnie almost ruined that case for us," he says.

"Bringing a TV station down there was certain to cause an uproar, and it was just a marketing stunt."

Bonnie laughed when she heard that. "*I* ruined *their* case? I'd been looking for those paintings for twenty years, and all they'd been looking for were reasons to quit. An FBI agent came to the gallery and told me I was on my own six years before Bob Wittman ever got involved. It wasn't *their* case. It was *our* case."

Bonnie recalls several phone calls from Wittman, as she and Gary were preparing to leave for Brazil. "He asked lots of questions about the theft, and he was very discouraging about our involvement in trying to get the paintings back. He kept pressing me for information. I was busy, and of course to the extent that I thought about it at all, I thought, 'Isn't it ironic that after all these years the FBI has developed this sudden interest in the case, and now they want me to drop everything I'm doing in order to help them.'"

An insurance investigator came to the gallery. "Wittman must have told him what we were up to because he knew all about it," Bonnie says. "I certainly didn't try to hide anything. He asked why we were going, and we told him."

The Lindbergs told a trusted friend about the visit, and at his recommendation they hired a criminal attorney, just in case.

The last call from Wittman came the day before Bonnie and her brother left for Brazil. "I wouldn't talk to him, I was so mad," she says.

The feeling was mutual, although they've both mellowed a bit since. Bonnie now gives Wittman credit for a level of resolve about the case that other investigators lacked. "He's done some tremendous work recovering stolen art," she says.

Wittman sticks by his claim that the TV coverage was designed to goose the market for the Date Paintings, but he doesn't dispute Bonnie's assertion that she stuck with the search long after the FBI gave up. He admits that he didn't go to work on the stolen Rockwells until Turak called him. He says he vaguely recalls the Detroit contacts from his review of the files but cautions that tipsters and purported go-betweens often contact the victims of art thefts, and they're usually scammers.

20

IN DECEMBER 1998, A PACKAGE WRAPPED IN BROWN paper arrived at Elayne Galleries.

"I was so excited I didn't take any notice of how it had been shipped," says Bonnie. "I think it entered the United States via international mail, and was forwarded to us in the parcel post."

Bonnie's arrangement with the TV station allowed them to film her opening the package. She had a hard time holding up her end. "I told them they'd better hurry, because I was in such a state that I didn't know if I could restrain myself."

But she did, and as a result there is a video record of her carefully pulling off the wrapping, and her eyes tearing up as she examines the painting Carneiro has sent—"Before the Date/Cowgirl"—and pronounces it authentic.

"My God," she says. "This is it!"

On December 24, 1998, $40,000 was wired to a bank

account in Miami, per Carneiro's instructions. Two weeks later Bonnie and Gary, Bonnie's husband Kevin, and a three-person crew from KARE 11 flew to Rio de Janeiro. They spent the first night at a hotel. The next morning Carneiro picked them up in a Land Rover and they set out for Teresopolis.

Their destination was in the heavily forested mountains north of the city, three thousand feet above the beaches of Rio. The road initially led them through mile after mile of hillside slums. Then the city ended abruptly, and the wilderness began.

Teresopolis wasn't far as the crow flies, but the highway wound circuitously, switchbacking up steep hills, then dropping into valleys thick with vine-covered trees. Flocks of brilliantly colored birds flashed across the road. In the distance they caught glimpses of two jagged and oddly shaped mountain peaks, Dedo de Deus (God's Finger) and Nariz do Frade (the Monk's Nose).

Remote as the area seemed, the road was well traveled. Summer was in full swing in the southern hemisphere, and Carneiro explained that Teresopolis was a favorite escape from the oppressive coastal heat, especially for the Carioca elite. It had been since Dom Pedro II, the last emperor of Brazil, made his summer residence there.

They stopped halfway, so Carneiro could buy everyone lunch. "It was this fabulous palace for carnivores," says Gary. "Jose was quite the host. He made sure we all gorged ourselves until we were practically comatose." After lunch they continued to Teresopolis, a town of about 100,000 people. Their first stop was an office building in which Carneiro's art gallery was located.

"This is my small gallery," he announced. "I have a much larger one in Lisbon." He asked the TV crew to refrain from filming while he showed them around.

"He had some interesting art," says Gary, "but he didn't say much about it. Instead he talked about his school, and how important it was to be educating the children of the community. It seemed to be his way of emphasizing what an upright citizen he was. We didn't stay at the gallery very long. 'Tonight I entertain you, tomorrow we'll look at art,' he said."

Nevertheless, after they arrived at Carneiro's Teresopolis residence, which took up the entire upper floor of an apartment building, they next spent more than an hour viewing all the paintings on display there. Carneiro's wife was friendly, but she didn't seem to know what all the hullabaloo was about and had no role in the entertainment. A chef had been hired to cook dinner—several courses, more meat.

"They eat an awful lot of meat down there," says Gary.

It was late evening by the time the dishes were cleared. Carneiro proposed a toast, then another. "I don't drink, so I had soda," says Gary, "but he seemed to be fortifying himself."

They discussed logistics for a while. Carneiro had made hotel arrangements for everyone. He said they would need an early start the next morning because they had a bit of a drive ahead of them. They would be heading to his villa, he explained. The television crew was welcome to come, but he had some second thoughts about filming.

"He'd gotten cold feet," says Gary, "which is what I'd been worried about. They'd taken a few atmospheric shots at that point, but the paintings were what they came to see."

Carneiro explained that he simply couldn't allow photographs of the art he kept there, or even of the place itself. It was past midnight by then. The crew was disappointed, and Bonnie and Kevin were glum. Gary said that he would stick around awhile and reason with Jose. The others could retire for the night.

"We talked until 4:00 AM," he says, "talked it all through. He kept drinking while I tried every argument I could. 'I'll tell you what I'm afraid of,' he said. 'I do business in the United States, and people there are going to see me, but they won't hear my message. I'll be the bad guy. I'll be blamed. Then it will get back here, my reputation will suffer, children will be pulled from my school and everything will come crashing down.' We went over every possible bad outcome, and I countered them with good ones. It took a long time, but eventually he agreed to go through with it."

A few hours later, the two-car caravan took off. It was another sixty-mile drive into the mountains before they arrived at Carneiro's gated villa.

Bonnie and Gary Lindberg with TV crew at Jose Carneiro's villa in the Brazilian mountains

Workers were busy on the grounds. Peacocks were strutting among the statues. A groomed trail led up the mountainside, through the rain forest. "It was paradise, just gorgeous," says Bonnie. "I wish I'd been in a better frame of mind to absorb it all, but I'd hardly slept and we were anxious to see the paintings."

Carneiro was in no rush, though. He insisted that they tour the estate. The camera crew filmed background shots for the series, while Carneiro explained the provenance of the statuary and the history of the property. Finally, an hour and a half later, they entered the villa for the first time, passed through a foyer into a kind of living room, and there on the wall hung the missing Rockwells.

"We actually gasped," says Bonnie. "It was kind of overwhelming. Twenty-one years we'd been wondering what had become of them, and suddenly there they were."

The cameras whirred as the paintings were taken off the wall for authentication, which was quick and conclusive. Several paintings still had "Elayne Galleries" stamped on the back of the canvas. Then it was time for an interview with Carneiro. He explained that he purchased the paintings legally and in good faith, and, in essence, he had been duped.

The deal for the second Date Painting had already

been struck. Carneiro promised he would send it as soon as the money arrived. That night the group was on a plane back to Minneapolis.

By the time the series aired on KARE 11, both Date Paintings were back in the hands of their rightful owner.

21

SPECIAL AGENT WITTMAN WATCHED A TAPE OF THE SERIES a few weeks later. The Twin Cities audience had seen a heartwarming tale of pluck and perseverance, but what Wittman saw was a public relations disaster for the FBI.

Part one went into detail about the Lindbergs' efforts and introduced Bonnie as the lead detective on a case that the FBI had abandoned decades ago. "For the last three years, all leads led to Rio," the announcer said, "and all the leads were rejected by the FBI."

Part two begins with Bonnie unwrapping the first painting, then cuts to Brazil and Carneiro's villa. The three Rockwells that Wittman wanted to recover can be seen clearly, but his hopes of retrieving them faded as he watched.

"Jose Carneiro says he's done everything properly to purchase the paintings, which appears to be true," says the announcer, "and while he's willing to let the paintings go, he wants his money first. So the question remains, what will it take to bring the remaining Rockwells back? Carneiro knows that possession is nine-tenths of ownership, and he has that locked away in Brazil."

Carneiro displayed the letter he received from the Art Loss Register stating that the Rockwells weren't on their list.

In his book, *Priceless: How I Went Undercover to Rescue the World's Stolen Treasures,* Wittman devotes a chapter to the effort to recover the remaining Rockwells. He characterizes the eighteen months after he saw the series as full of diplomatic and bureaucratic delays. The problems he describes shed some light on why the FBI closed the case and why they refused to revisit it on the basis of leads that came afterward.

Wittman refers to "the long-held law enforcement mentality that art crime isn't a priority." He says that U.S. Attorney's offices are routinely run by control freaks who think the best ideas come from the top down, not from the investigators who do the work. Prosecutors expect cases to conclude with arrests and prosecutions, and the FBI's role is to assist them. Recovery of stolen property, cultural or otherwise, is always secondary.

In the case of the theft from Elayne Galleries, the investigators in Minneapolis knew who the thieves were, but they couldn't gather enough evidence to prove it and decided that they never would. The fake art scam interested the Miami office until plans to make an arrest fell apart, then that was abandoned.

The mutual assistance treaty Wittman and Hall had been waiting on was signed in February 2001. Bureaucratic conflicts continued to stall things, but when the Brazilians approved their request to question Carneiro, the project finally moved forward. They were in the midst of preparations to leave for Rio on the morning of September 11, but their plans went up in smoke along with the World Trade Center towers.

The FBI sent Wittman to Ground Zero to counsel firefighters and law enforcement personnel. By the time he got back to Philadelphia, terrorism was such an overwhelming priority that their plans were in jeopardy again.

Ironically, it was the attacks of September 11 that ultimately sealed the deal for Wittman and Hall. One of the paintings Carneiro had, "The Spirit of 1976," is Rockwell's updated version of a nineteenth-century work depicting a fife and drum corps marching in front of an American flag. It was painted by Archibald MacNeal Willard in 1876. In Rockwell's painting, Boy Scouts are doing the marching, with a large flag fluttering behind them and the Manhattan skyline seen dimly in the background. The twin towers of the World Trade Center are faint, but unmistakable.

Hall pointed out this detail to a ranking prosecutor in his office, who recognized that recovering the painting could be a public relations coup. In December 2001, Wittman and Hall finally left for Rio. Their mission was the first under the new treaty and would constitute a test of its practical value.

In order to underline their new attitude of cooperation the Brazilian authorities had been pressuring Carneiro, but they weren't having much luck. Carneiro knew exactly where he stood legally—and financially. The treaty mandated cooperation, but it didn't supersede Brazilian law.

As for the paintings, their value had been climbing ever since he acquired them, and the events of September 11 had only fueled that trend. He was in the catbird seat. The two investigators weren't even sure they would be allowed to question him in person.

Hall had inquired about the possibility of extraditing Carneiro to face charges in the United States. That was unlikely, he was told. The federal prosecutor's office in Brazil did put Carneiro under investigation for failure to pay a national property tax when he bought the paintings. The penalty was a fine, not prison, but the investigation allowed the prosecutors to get a search warrant. They hoped to seize the paintings and turn them over to their U.S. counterparts.

Carneiro's villa was searched. The paintings were nowhere to be found. The prosecutors forced Carneiro to give a deposition. He admitted under oath that he was still in control of the paintings but refused to divulge their whereabouts.

Wittman and Hall were under strict constraints. According to Department of Justice rules, any offer Hall made could be construed as binding, so he had orders to dangle nothing more than a promise not to prosecute. Wittman's situation was the opposite. As a law enforcement officer he could make any threats or promises he pleased, but they would all be worthless.

They met in the office of the Brazilian prosecutors, who opened the proceedings by reminding Carneiro that he was still under investigation on the tax charge. He laughed and called that a nuisance. He wondered why they had asked him to come, if that was what they wanted to discuss.

Hall told him he was in a world of trouble because, according to U.S. law, he was in possession of stolen property. Hall said that if they failed to reach an agreement, he would ask for Carneiro's extradition and put him in prison.

That elicited another laugh from Carneiro. He indicated that an extradition request would simply mean he had to stay put in Brazil. He nodded toward the window, which had a nice view of the Rio de Janeiro skyline and the mountains beyond. If it came to that he would try to cope, he said.

Wittman saw that threats wouldn't work. He portrayed the problem as political and enlisted Carneiro's support in finding a solution that would make everybody happy. That would be just great, Carneiro replied, but I haven't heard anything that makes me happy yet.

Wittman appealed to his self-interest, reminding him that the paintings weren't worth much in Brazil. They were worth plenty in the United States, he observed, but Carneiro couldn't sell them there. Then he accused Carneiro of holding the paintings hostage against America.

That hit a nerve. Carneiro protested that he loved America. Wittman countered that he wasn't making any friends there by refusing to repatriate the work of an iconic American artist, especially in view of the September 11 attacks. At that, they broke off for the day.

At their next meeting, Carneiro stated his price: $300,000 and a promise that he wouldn't be arrested if he came to the United States.

You aren't negotiating with the U.S. Treasury, Hall cautioned. But he said he and Wittman could act as middlemen if Carneiro wanted to deal with a party that might be willing to part with a reasonable sum.

Some serious haggling began. According to Wittman, it took several hours and many phone calls to St. Paul before there was an agreement. Carneiro would receive $100,000 from Brown & Bigelow, plus Hall's written promise that he would not face charges in the United States. The money would be sent by wire. As soon as it arrived, Carneiro would lead them to the paintings.

The next day the deal was consummated. Wittman and Hall retraced the Lindbergs' journey to Teresopolis. The paintings were hidden in Carneiro's school. He asked the Americans to examine them and take note of how carefully they had been handled. They were in good shape, Wittman agreed.

Before they left town, Hall called the embassy and asked for help getting on the next possible flight, as well as clearance through customs and security with the three large packages they would be carrying. By morning, the last of the stolen Rockwells were back in the United States.

The recovery was well publicized. The U.S. Attorney's office sent out a five-page press release. It summarized the theft and the case, skipped over years of investigatory inaction, and avoided naming the gallery owners or referencing their efforts. The FBI agent and the assistant U.S. Attorney who recovered the paintings went unnamed as well. Quite a bit of information about Carneiro, Rockwell, and each of the paintings was included.

The release ended with a quote from Attorney General John Ashcroft, who recognized the FBI and the U.S. Attorney for their "relentless pursuit of those in the criminal trade."

A few days later, the paintings were displayed at a news conference. U.S. Attorney Patrick Meehan called Rockwell "that most American of artists" and said recovery of the paintings was "very important for the American psyche at this time." He pointed out the faint image of the World Trade Center's twin towers in "The Spirit of 1976" and noted that the marching Boy Scouts came from Edison, New Jersey, not so far from Philadelphia, birthplace of the nation and home of the Liberty Bell.

A flurry of newspaper articles followed. There was one more photo op at the Minneapolis FBI office before the paintings were handed over to Brown & Bigelow on February 12, 2002.

There was no mention in the news, or in any of the DOJ's well-orchestrated publicity, of the $100,000 Brown & Bigelow paid to get the paintings back.

22

THE FINAL ACT FOR BONNIE LINDBERG HAD COME THREE years earlier. In the spring of 1999, she had plans to feature the well-traveled Date Paintings in a Welcome Home show at Elayne Galleries. The timing couldn't have been better. Rockwell's star was on the rise. The twenty-year odyssey of the paintings had been featured on TV and trumpeted in newspaper articles. Best of all, serious Rockwell collectors were on notice that "Before the Date/Cowgirl" had special value because it marked a turning point in the artist's career.

Karal Ann Marling, an art historian at the University of Minnesota, had written a book that placed Rockwell at the forefront of the realist tradition in American art. In February 1999, the *Minneapolis Tribune* sought Marling's opinion of the stolen Rockwells and their standing in the artist's canon. According to her, a little-known flap involving "Before the Date/ Cowgirl" turned out to be the beginning of the end of Rockwell's lengthy relationship with the *Saturday Evening Post.*

The paintings the gallery recovered were an early study for a *Post* cover. In an interview about his association with the magazine, Rockwell said that after he gave them the final version, "some hack" had been hired to make the cowgirl less racy. In the gallery's painting she is bent ever so slightly in front of a mirror, and some skin is showing through her slip. In the later version, the slip has lost its translucence.

According to Rockwell, that was the last straw. He

Russ, Bonnie, and her husband Kevin at the Welcome Home showing of the Date Paintings in 1999

was weary of battles with magazine editors who were determined to impose their middlebrow values on his work, and he quit painting covers for the *Post* in 1969. Marling told the *Tribune* that because of that incident and its effect on Rockwell's career, the Date Paintings were the most significant of the seven.

About the same time that the *Tribune* was quoting Marling, a collection of Rockwell's work embarked on a six-museum tour that included shows at the Chicago Historical Society, the San Diego Museum of Art, and the Corcoran Gallery of Art in Washington, DC, that raised the artist's profile considerably.

Shortly before the Welcome Home show at Elayne Galleries was scheduled to open, Bonnie got a call from Bruce Hanley, the criminal attorney she had hired before the trip to Brazil. Hanley said he had just spoken to the FBI.

"We have to go down and talk to them, right now," he said. "Otherwise they'll come and confiscate the paintings. I'll meet you there [at the FBI office]."

"I didn't know what was going on," says Bonnie.

Two agents were waiting, along with the insurance investigator who had stopped by before the trip to Brazil. They went into a conference room, where the agents took turns walking her through the entire story of their efforts to retrieve the paintings.

"I wondered what they were up to," says Bonnie. "I especially wondered why they were going over things I'd told them about already. I think I'd either talked to Bob Wittman or someone at the Minneapolis office every day in the week or two before we left for Brazil."

The good-guy agent asked what they had discussed with Carneiro in New York and how the deal went down in Brazil. He nodded with seeming approval when Bonnie told about the photos they had demanded and the way they had recovered one painting before any cash changed hands.

The bad-guy agent demanded to know why Bonnie thought they were entitled to keep the paintings.

"I said they were ours because we'd never gotten any insurance settlement on them," Bonnie says. "Then, he laid a piece of paper on the table—*bang!*—and asked if we'd seen it before."

It was a statement memorializing an insurance payment of $34,500 to the gallery for the loss of the two Date Paintings, signed by Elayne Lindberg.

"I just saw the whole twenty-year search coming to nothing," says Bonnie. "I almost broke down in tears, but instead I got angry. I told them I knew nothing about that payment. I'd asked for every single insurance document, more than once, and I'd never seen that one. I'd asked back when we heard from the guy in Argentina, I'd asked when we heard from Luis Palma, and again before we went to Brazil. 'Now you show me this!' I said. 'What kind of scam are you pulling?'"

Didn't we send you this? asked the insurance investigator. That must be because it was a different claim number.

He proceeded to explain that the records of the two payments, one to Brown & Bigelow, one to Elayne Galleries, must have been separated, possibly when the insurance company was sold. He called it an oversight and didn't seem to think it mattered much, because the payment had surely been made and acknowledged with Elayne Lindberg's signature.

But the FBI agents seemed to be taken aback by his admission. "I could tell they believed I'd never seen that document," says Bonnie. "That changed the tone of things. There was never any mention of stolen property after that."

The FBI took possession of the paintings pending a resolution of ownership. The Welcome Home show was postponed. A few weeks later Hanley suggested a way to move forward, and the insurer's attorney agreed. The gallery would put $34,500 in escrow. The paintings would be released to the gallery. Home Insurance would sue, and the court would decide who got what.

Hanley bowed out at that point, and Daniel Taber, a litigator, took over.

Home Insurance argued that according to an insurer's right of subrogation (the right to pursue a party that caused an insurance loss for the amount of the claim), it should get its money back, or the paintings, or both.

Taber argued that Minnesota law does not allow an insurer to enforce its subrogation rights until the insured has been made whole. In this case the insured had paid $80,000 to Carneiro to get the paintings back, plus an estimated $30,000 in expenses searching for the paintings.

Secondly, he argued, the paintings were not recovered through any claim of right by the insured, because according to Brazilian law Carneiro was the rightful owner. Since the insured had no right to the paintings, the insurer had no rights as subrogee.

In a court filing, Taber wrote, "Words on paper are woefully insufficient to express the outrageous nature of any such claims as the insurer's. The gallery is irrefutably entitled to the paintings with no obligation to reimburse Home's payment of $34,500. . . . The gallery needed the entire $34,500, plus another $45,000, to buy back the paintings. If the gallery now had to pay Home $34,500, the insurer would become the insured and the insured the insurer. The gallery would end up with an $80,000 loss with nothing from Home. On the other hand, Home would end up with no loss, having been paid in full by the gallery. Such a result would not only be inequitable, it would be absurd."

The court agreed. The judge's ruling in favor of the gallery had some harsh words for the insurer. He noted that they sat back and watched without lifting a finger while the Lindbergs spent more than twenty years searching for the paintings, and then expected to be rewarded for their lack of effort. Neither time nor money had been invested by the insurer, and therefore it had no claim on the fruits of what had been a monumental effort.

The Welcome Home show was finally held, and it was a great success. There were big crowds, lots of coverage by local TV stations, and a story by the Associated Press that was picked up by several newspapers around the country.

In November 1999, the Date Paintings were sold through a New York auction house for $180,000.

In 2001, Bonnie closed Elayne Galleries. The boom times for art as an investment were past. There were still steady sales to collectors, but an offer to buy the building came along and she took it. She and her husband went into the appraisal business.

"Appraisal was always the part we liked best," she says. Now she does her searching on the Internet.

Her memories of the days when she was fielding tips, trying to make deals with shady characters, and wondering whether the FBI saw her as someone they wanted to help or someone they wanted to arrest—all have grown fonder over the years.

"It was hard, it was frustrating, it was full of disappointments, but ultimately it was rewarding. Especially because everybody got their paintings back, not just us. And it was exciting too, no question. You know, the first thing you think when you find out you've been robbed is, 'I wish that hadn't happened,' but looking back on it now, if I had it all to do over, I wouldn't change a thing. It was an adventure. A real one. How many of those do you get in your life?"

In 2011, she attended a lecture at the Minneapolis Institute of Arts about recovering stolen art. The speaker was Bob Wittman. His book had been published the year before, and he was on an author's tour. The event was well attended, and people were eager to talk to Wittman afterward. Bonnie wanted to introduce herself, but she ended up near the end of a long line of people waiting to get copies of his book signed.

She was about to give up when he glanced her way and said, "Hi, Bonnie. Hang on, I'll be right with you."

She found it unnerving that after all those years, and having never met him face to face, he recognized her. They must have photos of me, she thought, maybe even recent ones. It made her wonder how much of a "person of interest" she had been. Or maybe still was.

They had a nice chat, but she didn't buy his book.

Note on Sources

THIS BOOK RELIES HEAVILY ON THE RECOLLECTIONS OF Bonnie and Gary Lindberg, who are quoted liberally in the text. Many thanks to them, and to Minneapolis attorney Thomas Bauer, who opened some doors that might have remained closed otherwise.

Two books that were referenced in the text, *The Irish Game: A True Story of Crime and Art* by Matthew Hart and *The Rescue Artist: A True Story of Art, Thieves, and the Hunt for a Missing Masterpiece* by Edward Dolnick, were informative about the stolen art market and the Irish gangster Martin Cahill, who is discussed in both. Robert K. Wittman's book, *Priceless: How I Went Undercover to Rescue the World's Stolen Treasures,* was especially useful in respect to the recovery of the stolen paintings.

The FBI's files on its investigation of the theft from

Elayne Galleries were invaluable, even the parts that were "redacted." Minneapolis attorney Joe Friedberg was helpful, and so were many other sources, most named but some who preferred to remain anonymous. Among the latter, the tipster who wouldn't stop tipping stands out. Thank you, whoever you are.